Be kind

Kindness Matters.

PRAISE FOR
THE BUSINESS CASE FOR KINDNESS

As president of our women's organization, I'm always looking for talented, enthusiastic people. When I met Cherie Crim, I knew I'd hit the jackpot. Cherie is not only talented and enthusiastic, but intelligent, energetic, kind, considerate, thoughtful, and passionate about our shared causes. Cherie is the one who always volunteers for any task but follows through and shows up! She's the first one there and the last to leave! She truly cares about people and wants the best for them! Her word is her bond and she doesn't let you down! She's a great speaker and she presents her material like a pro. If Cherie wants you to feel something, you most definitely will. It's not every day you find someone like Cherie Crim, but when you do, hold on tight because she's the real deal!

—Candice Burgess

It is a rare pleasure in life to meet a leader like Cherie Crim. She employs her passionate energy, persistence, and fortitude to the service of speaking truth to power in order to make you and the world around you a better place. Her inspiring presence transforms and improves every organization she is a part of by confidently breaking down the tyranny of low expectations and mediocre results. Cherie and her unflappable style calls all of us to better performance and a higher purpose in business and activism.

—JP Ferreira

I've had the pleasure of working with Cherie indirectly and directly over the years. She sets the bar high based on her role-modeling behavior. She has always made business decisions with business goals in mind as well as with her coworkers and team members in mind. Cherie is a natural leader.

—*Valerie Kelley*

Cherie Crim is like a breath of fresh air in the fight for social justice and civil rights. Always respecting the individual, she is fierce and steady in her ability to get things done and effectuate positive change. As a leader and teacher, Cherie is undeniably a forward-thinking socio-political force.

—*Ron Demkowski*

I have worked with Cherie on multiple projects and organizing events over the last three years and she has the willingness and ability to do whatever it takes to make them happen. She promotes the cause—not her own self-interest—and takes direction as well as she gives it. She is a flexible problem-solver who always follows through. Cherie is thoughtful, caring, and organized and this carries over to her leadership style. It is always a pleasure to work with her.

—*Laura Bjorklund*

Cherie is a leader not because of a title. She is a leader because she is willing to dedicate herself to helping others to grow and learn. Her passion for a more equitable and inclusive society drives her daily as she gives voice to the voiceless in our community. She will touch many lives for years to come.

—*Beverly*

THE BUSINESS CASE
FOR KINDNESS

THE BUSINESS CASE
FOR KINDNESS

HOW KINDNESS, RESPECT & TRUST HOLD THE POWER TO TRANSFORM CORPORATE AMERICA

Cherie Crim

PUBLISH
YOUR
PURPOSE
PRESS

Publish Your Purpose Press
141 Weston Street, #155
Hartford, CT, 06141

PUBLISH
YOUR
PURPOSE
PRESS

The opinions expressed by the Author are not necessarily those held by Publish Your Purpose Press.

Ordering Information: Quantity sales and special discounts are available on quantity purchases by corporations, associations, and others. For details, contact the publisher at orders@publishyourpurposepress.com.

Cover design by: Alexander Vulchev
Typeset by: Medlar Publishing Solutions Pvt Ltd., India

Printed in the United States of America.
ISBN: 978-1-946384-74-4 (paperback)
ISBN: 978-1-946384-75-1 (hardcover)
ISBN: 978-1-946384-76-8 (ebook)

Library of Congress Control Number: 2019908394

First edition, November 2019.

Publish Your Purpose Press works with authors, and aspiring authors, who have a story to tell and a brand to build. Do you have a book idea you would like us to consider publishing? Please visit PublishYourPurposePress.com for more information.

DEDICATION

For my chosen family

TABLE OF CONTENTS

A LETTER FROM THE AUTHOR

On February 26, 2015, I gave my two weeks' notice at my big corporate job. Within one day of that notice, I was told my last day would be March 1. I was trying to do the right thing, but they decided they didn't want to pay me for my last two weeks. They dated all my paperwork for February 28, 2015, instead of the March 1 date, which took away my health insurance. A fact that I didn't know until almost three weeks later when I got a letter from my insurance provider. These types of behaviors (bad and illegal) have been happening for too long. We have come to accept that this type of behavior is normal. IT IS NOT. Welcome to the Business Case for Kindness.

I have structured this book into two main sections. The First Part (Chapters 1 through 3) is where the research, data, and analysis are located. The Second Part (Chapters 4 through 6) is where you will learn about the KRT model, must-have leadership skills, and business case cost/benefit model examples. I have written many business cases, instructional guides, and methods and procedures for all levels of employees. While writing these I learned what worked well and what didn't work at all. I have incorporated this expertise into my book.

In each section you will learn the key facts that build on each other to provide the entire picture. You will read about real examples of what is being discussed. You will learn definitions, see key callouts, and get decades of research and information. The entirety of this information will lead to one main conclusion. *We must change for our future.*

Now is the time to understand the generational changes that both the millennials and Generation Z are bringing to the marketplace. This paradigm shift is coming, and those who don't change their business models will have a difficult time surviving in the future.

I get it, I know we are told that change is scary, and we don't like it. But what if I told you this change is going to make you happier, healthier, and more productive? This change will not only help businesses but also families, communities, and individuals. Making the changes discussed in this book can be the pivotal turning point that we desperately need within our world. With this in mind, I created the KRT model to help lead us into the future.

So, what is this KRT model? It is very simple: Kindness, Respect, and Trust. Think about it as a pyramid. Kindness is the bottom level, Respect is the middle level, and Trust is at the top. Just like Maslow's Hierarchy of Needs, we must build from the bottom up.

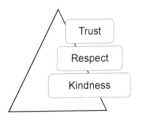

At the end of each chapter, I will bring us back to the main points of the KRT model and how they relate to that chapter. Chapters 1 and 2 will give you information on how we got to this point in business and how we have normalized many bad behaviors. Chapter 3 will dive into how the data fits completely into the KRT model. Building on Chapters 1 through 3, Chapter 4 will go deep into the KRT model. Chapter 5 will give you must-have leadership skills to help you create the environment of kindness that your business needs. Chapter 6 shows the business case cost/benefit model and how this model will always lead to increases in profit. Lastly, in Chapter 7, we recap what we have learned and what you can do for the future.

Are you ready to go on this kindness journey with me?

INTRODUCTION

What if I told you this book can do the following for your company?

- Increase sales
- Decrease employee turnover
- Increase customer satisfaction
- Decrease lawsuits

Wouldn't you want to know how?

I am a reformed Fortune 10 Director who saw all the good, bad, ugly, illegal, immoral, and just plain stupid business practices that Corporate America believes is normal. These practices have helped contribute to enormous income inequality that hasn't been seen in the U.S. for almost 100 years. I helped by finding efficiencies and working for a company that surplused employees every year I worked there. Jobs that made over $50K to $60K a year (in 2000) now make around $25K to $35K because of outsourcing and job description changes. Employees are being expected to handle multiple people's jobs and when they cannot they are labeled as incompetent.

I remember the day I took on the jobs of two people, then three, then four people's jobs at an introductory management level. I did not get paid overtime while the entire time Human Resources and my managers were telling me that this was ok. This happened every time I was promoted. This is the truth of how employees are being treated in all job levels. Companies keep adding responsibilities but never think about the overall effect on the employee.

Why have we allowed this type of behavior to become normalized?

How did the U. S. become a country that is run by greed, fear, and hatred?

In the name of capitalism and our greed, we have created a society that has become an apathetic instant gratification nation. We don't care, but we want everything as fast as possible. This attitude we have has enabled the pay gap for women, LGBTQ+, and people of color and unneeded tax breaks for companies and the wealthiest Americans. We are at a critical point in our history and we can choose the path forward.

I want to be clear that capitalism isn't the problem by itself. The problem is that we have allowed selfishness (the greed is good mentality) to become the norm. We believe that corporations must maximize value for shareholders. We believe that employee pay must be as low as possible to make more money for the company. We stopped valuing employees all in the name of greed. *It's time we change the narrative.*

We have allowed industries to become monopolized by only a few companies. The wireless industry is controlled by just three companies. Around 90% of all customers have either T-Mobile/Sprint, Verizon, or AT&T. The pharmacy industry is controlled by just three companies, as well. Approximately, 90% of customers use CVS, Walgreens, or Rite Aid. Why do we think this lack of competition is ok?

Imagine if your company was transparent on salaries and benefits, do you think the company would be a good place to work? Buc-ee's, a Texas-based convenience store chain, does just that. They have a sign at every store showing how they pay. In fact, they pay way above minimum wage and offer 40+-hour work weeks, 401k benefits, and paid time off that you can use, cash, or roll over. They are transparent and treat employees as more than just a number. They know their employees work hard helping customers, are on their feet all day, and want to compensate them for their hard work.

The example above is not the norm, though. The norm is companies hiding salary information, laying off employees yearly, treating employees like numbers, and allowing all the bad behaviors. If you aren't outraged at what is happening right now, then you are not paying attention. It is time to wake up.

Woke: To have social awareness of what is really going on

Both you and I have a choice to make just like in the movie the *Matrix*. Neo was given a choice between taking the red pill or the blue pill.

Red pill: Truth of reality, knowledge, freedom, and adversity

Blue pill: Blissful ignorance of illusion and falsehoods, security, and perceived happiness

These two constructs are a perfect representation for understanding how people can live their lives. We can choose to take the red pill and become woke or we can choose to take the blue pill and live in blissful ignorance and deny the truth. I remember the day I woke up; I was heartbroken to learn the life I was living was an illusion, full of corruption and lies that I had justified as normal. I wasn't living my life with purpose. I was living my life to make the most amount of money and to get to the highest position possible. I was living the greed-is-good mentality. Once I woke up to the truth, I realized I could not go back to the corporate world. I decided that I had to be part of the change and expose the truth.

For my entire career, corporations have allowed all the bad behaviors including discrimination, bigotry, Adult Bullies, and bad business practices to continue all in the name of making more money at any cost. They have been using the Don't Ask, Don't Tell methodology along with command and control (strict father morality) culture. Society has allowed the degradation and cultural gaslighting of an entire generation (millennials) because they are showing us that it is time to change. We have become so afraid of the change that it's just easier to blame millennials for being lazy and entitled. Why should we look at the whole picture? Can we see through all the lies that we have been taught are normal?

We are teetering between: The old command and control (strict father figure) culture vs. the nurturing (equity/equality) culture. This is a cultural shift that I have not seen before in my lifetime.

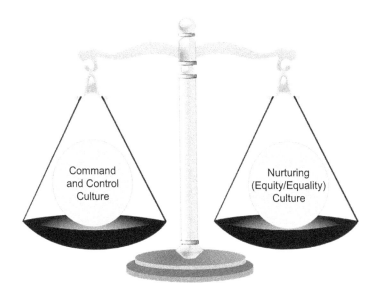

This book is dedicated to the whole picture—including the good, bad, and very ugly. Are you ready to face the truth and make the changes needed to thrive in business and in your life? The bad practices need to be abandoned for the greater good. The Adult Bullies need to be held accountable for their behavior because business is not high school. Cheaters need to face the reality that cheaters don't win. If managers want to succeed, they will need to learn to become leaders.

Times are changing and to survive, companies will need to change from the top down. It all starts with you and me having the courageous conversations with coworkers, friends, and family about the discrimination, unequal pay, hostile work environments, and many more bad behaviors. Just because you personally don't see or feel the discrimination does not mean that it isn't there. If one person is seeing it, then it is a problem. We need to stop blaming the victims and using bias/stereotypes and start listening to each other. Confront the issues head-on and have productive conversations. Let's learn from each other to take business to the next level and create inclusive, diverse, and psychologically safe environments. This is our future. Companies that don't step up and embrace the changes needed will not be around for much longer.

Some would rather stay in their bubble (take the blue pill) and pretend that these bad behaviors aren't happening or don't exist. They would rather blame the victim and make them feel like they caused the issue, instead of looking at the real issue: the perpetrator. How did we become so self-absorbed that we stopped caring about our fellow humans? Somewhere mixed with all the greed and need for material things, we have lost our empathy.

> **Empathy:** The action of understanding, being aware of, being sensitive to, and vicariously experiencing the feelings, thoughts, and experience of another of either the past or present without having the feelings, thoughts, and experience fully communicated in an objectively explicit manner.

Empathy is undervalued. Being able to place yourself in another person's shoes is scary and uncomfortable but will lead to the truth. Empathy is especially hard for people who are privileged because of money, skin color, and social status (including Adult Bullies). *We, the people, are lacking empathy.* We would rather blame the victim of sexual assault or harassment than blame the perpetrator. Is it any wonder that people don't report these types of crimes? In fact, some police departments cared so little about rape kit testing, they stopped testing the kits to save money in their budget. At one point, there were up to hundreds of thousands of rape kits that were not tested.[1] This is the truth of the world we live in right now.

Think about how different our world would be if we acted and thought in a more positive and empathetic way. Imagine what nudges of compassion and bumps of empathy could do for our communities and our society. It's no wonder we have so much violence when we have forgotten what it is like to be kind to one another. We have forgotten what it is like to respect another person's opinion or thoughts. It's time to undo the greed-is-good attitude that we have come to know as normal. It's time we stop hiding from the truth.

As of 2019, and per our laws, it is illegal to pay men more than women, but just read the news and you will see the pay gap is anywhere from 10% to 30%. In fact, in 2019 Citibank had to reveal that it has a gap of 29% for women.[2] It's time for innovative ideas like independent pay audits to be implemented so that we can move ahead and start fixing the pay gap.

The U.S. is made of immigrants who believe in the American dream. Why do people feel that we need to discriminate against others? How is it appropriate that slavery is still alive and well (in the form of the prison system)? Why are men (mostly white) making laws around women's reproductive rights? When did facts and science become "fake news"?

---

[1] Dickson, "Rape kits."
[2] McGregor, "Citigroup."

It is time to look ahead and become the leaders that we need in this world. Change is possible when we all see the truth of the situation. The examples in this book are actual, real experiences. The names have been changed to help protect the employees of the companies. These examples will show a true picture of what is going on in the business world.

KRT Inaction—Bad management example

Cory was one of my top managers, he had amazing knowledge and could find a solution when we didn't have the systems that we needed to make things work. Cory left my team in July and went to a new job within the company. I was so happy that he had gotten this job and helped with the transition. He helped me hire the most qualified person for his replacement.

In February, when my company did its yearly reviews, Cory called me to tell me he was rated "meets some of his goals." His budget was taken away and most of his projects were canceled. One of my top employees who exceeded all goals was now being rated where he could not get a bonus. I did not understand, so I had to call his new manager. She was no help and didn't see the problem. In fact, most of the team member's projects were canceled, so why weren't they all rated the same?

I emailed my manager and Human Resources to let them know what was going on. The last line of my email was "We are going to lose a high-potential manager from ***** due to this treatment." They would not help. They told me to have Cory talk to his manager, which, of course, did not help. A few months later, Cory left the company because of such discriminatory behavior by his manager and got a promotion at another business.

KRT Recap

Both Cory's manager and Human Resources were treating Cory like a number and not like the excellent employee that he was. His manager never made his success her goal. If the KRT model was being used, she would have taken into consideration his work for the entire year and not just when he was with her.

PART I

1

HOW WE GOT HERE

BACKGROUND AND DEFINITIONS

Trust. A big word. In business, trust is what makes or breaks the big project or company. Trust is not given away for free. Trust is earned, and once that trust is broken, it is extremely hard to recover. We are entering a new era in business where trust is more important than ever in retaining employees. There can be no trust without the truth.

> *"The truth is a virus"*
>
> ***Pump Up the Volume* (1990)**
> Movie

I am a firm believer of pulling off the Band-Aid and getting down to business. Before we can do that, we need to visit some important definitions and dates in history. Now, more than ever, it's critical that we learn everything we can because we are backsliding.

This background is important because we must make sure we know the right terms and information from the past to see where we need to go in the future:

Adult Bully: One who is habitually cruel to others who are weaker, smaller, or in some way vulnerable.

Bigotry: Obstinate or intolerant devotion to one's own opinions and prejudices.

Business Case: Provides justification for undertaking a project or program. It evaluates the benefit, cost, and risk of alternative options and provides a rationale for the preferred solution.

Capitalism: An economic and political system in which a country's trade and industry are controlled by private owners for profit, rather than by the state.

Code of Honor: A set of rules or ethical principles governing a business/community based on ideals that define what constitutes acceptable behavior within that business/community.

Cognitive Dissonance: The mental discomfort (psychological stress) experienced by a person who holds two or more contradictory beliefs, ideas, or values.

Company Culture: The personality of a company. It defines the environment in which employees work. Company culture includes a variety of elements, including work environment, company mission, value, ethics, expectations, and goals.

Confirmation Bias: The tendency to search for, interpret, favor, and recall information in a way that confirms one's preexisting beliefs or hypotheses.

Corporate Social Responsibility (CSR): Also called corporate conscience, corporate citizenship, or responsible business. A form of corporate self-regulation integrated into a business model. CSR policy functions as a self-regulatory mechanism whereby a business monitors and ensures its active compliance with the spirit of the law, ethical standards, and national or international norms.

Discrimination: The unjust or prejudicial treatment of different categories of people or things; especially on the grounds of race, age, and sex.

Gaslighting: A form of mental abuse in which information is twisted, spun, or selectively omitted to favor the abuser or false information is presented with the intent of making victims doubt their own memory, perception, and sanity.

Gratitude: The quality of being thankful; readiness to show appreciation for and to return kindness.

Greed: A selfish desire to have more of something (especially money).

Hostile Work Environment: Exists when one's behavior within a workplace creates an environment that is difficult for another person to work in.

Human Rights Ordinance (HRO): A policy passed on the local level (city or county) to prohibit discrimination based on certain characteristics. These policies often ban discrimination in housing, public accommodations, and employment.

Human Trafficking: The trade of humans for the purpose of forced labor, sexual slavery, or commercial sexual exploitation for the trafficker or others. This may encompass providing a spouse in the context of forced marriage or the extraction of organs or tissues. Human trafficking can occur within a country or trans-nationally. Human trafficking is a crime against the person because of the violation of the victim's rights of movement through coercion and because of their commercial exploitation.

Human trafficking is the trade in people, especially women and children, and does not necessarily involve the movement of the person from one place to another.

Implicit Bias: An attitude that always favors one way of feeling or acting especially without considering any other possibilities.

Income Inequality: The unequal distribution of household or individual income across the various participants in an economy.

Leader: A person who rules, guides, or inspires others; head.

Microaggression: Brief, commonplace, or daily verbal, behavioral, or environmental indignities, whether intentional or unintentional, that communicate hostile, derogatory, or negative prejudicial slights and insults toward any group.

Misogyny: A hatred of women.

Pay Audit: Comparing the pay of all people doing equal work in your organization. An audit is not simply a data collection exercise. It entails a commitment to put right any unfair pay inequalities.

Prejudice: An irrational attitude of hostility directed against an individual, a group, a race, or their supposed characteristics.

Privileged: Having special rights or advantages that most people do not have.

Racism: Racial prejudice or discrimination.

Sexism: Discrimination based on gender, especially against women.

Sexual Harassment: Uninvited and unwelcome verbal or physical behavior of a sexual nature, especially by a person in authority toward a subordinate (such as an employee or student).

Stereotype: To believe unfairly that all people or things with a particular characteristic are the same.

Toxic Masculinity: The socially constructed attitudes that describe the masculine gender role as violent, unemotional, sexually aggressive, and these traits are normal.

Unconscious Bias: When discrimination and incorrect judgments occur due to stereotyping. These can occur automatically and without the person being aware of it.

Generations

- **Baby Boomers:** Born from 1946 to 1964
- **Generation X:** Born in the early 1960s to early 1980s
- **Generation Y (millennials):** Born in the early 1980s to early 2000s
- **Generation Z:** Born in the early 2000s to present

Important Dates in History

- 1920—Women gained the right to vote, almost a full 100 years after men. (Did not include black women or Native American women.)
- 1963—Guaranteed equal pay to women for equal work (Equal Pay Act).
- 1964—Civil Rights Act (black people gained the right to vote 44 years after women).
- 1965—Voting Rights Act (making the voting rights promised by the Nineteenth Amendment a reality for women of color who had been disenfranchised through discriminatory voting laws).
- 1969—Stonewall Raid—Protests and demonstrations begin. This become the impetus for the gay civil rights movement.

- 1974—Illegal to discriminate in terms of credit opportunities based on such things as gender, marital status, race, religion, age, nation of birth, or proper residence.
- 1982—Parents and Friends of Lesbians and Gays (PFLAG) goes national.
- 1993—Bill Clinton signs "Don't Ask, Don't Tell" (Department of Defense Directive 1304.26).
- 2003—U.S. Supreme Court strikes down the "homosexual conduct" law.
- 2004—First legal same-sex marriage in Massachusetts.
- 2011— "Don't ask, Don't Tell" is ended.
- 2015—U.S. Supreme Court rules that states cannot ban same-sex marriage.
- 2019—Trump's Transgender Military Ban goes into effect

As you can see, women, people of color, and people of different sexual orientation *have always* been treated differently (discriminated against) in the U.S. compared to white straight males.

Stop
Discrimination

Did you know the U.S. never passed the Equal Rights Amendment (ERA)? Seriously, in 1972 only 22 of the 38 states necessary for ratification voted for the ERA.

What is the ERA? It is a proposed amendment to the U. S. Constitution designed to guarantee equal rights for all citizens regardless of sex. It seeks to end the legal distinctions between men and women in terms of divorce, property, employment, and other matters.

The ERA is still introduced in every session of Congress because it is important. On March 22, 2017, 45 years to the day after Congress passed the ERA, Nevada became the 36ᵗʰ state to ratify it. Then on May 30, 2018, Illinois passed the ERA. **As of September 2019, there are still 13 states that have not ratified the ERA.** Those states are:

- Alabama
- Arizona
- Arkansas
- Florida
- Georgia
- Louisiana
- Mississippi
- Missouri
- North Carolina
- Oklahoma
- South Carolina
- Utah
- Virginia

Check out the author lobbying in Florida for ERA in 2019 www.bekindtoall.com

In 2017, Florida held meetings throughout the state with the Constitution Revision Commission. They asked Florida's citizens what amendments the state should look at. I, as well as hundreds of women across the state, asked for the ERA to be passed for Florida. I vividly remember the day I spoke in front of the commission. I was wearing my rainbow flag and thinking, "Will they even listen to what I have to say?" Well, that answer became clear immediately. While I was presenting during the two to three minutes I was given, as soon as I said, "equal rights," I saw all of the men look down and the majority of the women, too. Why even hold these meetings if you aren't even going to pretend to give a shit?

Let's not forget that there are no federal statutes explicitly addressing employee discrimination based on sexual orientation or gender identity. Twenty states plus D.C., Guam, and Puerto Rico have statutes that protect against both sexual orientation and gender identity discrimination.

The point is that we still have a lot of work to do to get to equal rights for all.

MILLENNIALS ARE THE FUTURE

It is time for a historical shift in how businesses are operated. Millennials are showing the rest of the workforce that the status quo of business operations is obsolete and they don't want to work for companies that treat employees as expendable. They have found all the discriminations, flaws, inappropriate behaviors, and dishonest interactions and are exposing them. The problem is that employers don't like change and don't think they should change.

Millennials are the majority of the workforce.

Generation X (my generation) has learned from the baby boomers and has allowed all the bad behaviors to continue in business. This whole concept of command and control, getting in line, and following orders is outdated. Businesses now need step up and create cultures that engage and cultivate their employees.

"The baby boomers inherited a rich, dynamic country and have gradually bankrupted it," according to a *Vox* article "How the baby boomers—not millennials—screwed America."[3] The facts are very clear. The gross debt–to-GDP ratio was 35% in 1975 and now it is 103%. Boomers have continued to disregard facts and choose their feelings about matters such as climate change, gun reform, and immigration. Or did they choose this path because of greed because we know that trickle-down economics does not work? Did you know that the top 1% of Americans have as much money as the bottom 82%. The only way to change our path is to stop allowing the greed of the 1% to run our country.

Before we go any further, we need to look at the different generations. Each generation has its own characteristics indicative of the time period that its members grew up in. These differences are important to note, especially because the millennials are the majority of the workforce. Below is a chart showing the differences.

Generational Matrix:

	Boomers	Gen X	Millennials (Gen Y)
Trust for authority	Confident of self, not authority	Low level	High level for authority but low level of trust for individual people
Rewards	Want the title and office	Freedom	Meaningful work
Political	Attack oppression	Apathetic and worried about the individual	Crave community and involvement

Inc.'s article "Why are Millennials So Unhappy at Work?" states that "the disparity between expectation and reality is the

---

[3] Illing, "Baby boomers."

reason behind millennials' unhappiness and their lack of engagement of work."[4] They believe that millennials weren't ready for rejection and they are bombarded with their peers' success. This is true of any generation. Isn't it time we stop playing the blame game and work toward solutions?

The younger generations (millennials/generation Z) are challenging and questioning the why behind everything. This comes from their self-awareness and as we learn the truth we cannot hide and sweep this truth under the rug. As we have always done in our society, we allow age discrimination in the workplace, whether it is younger or older discrimination. We would rather hold onto our stereotypes/biases than see what is right there in front of our eyes. It's time we stop living in our bubbles and see the truth.

What makes millennials special?

- They are more diverse and tolerant of races and groups than any other generation.
- They expect equal opportunity and want hard projects.
- They are offended because they are tired of seeing people of color punished because of systemic racism.
- They are multitaskers, are passionate, and don't want to follow others' paths.
- They were raised on praise, which leads to them to be driven by recognition.
- They are generous and take care of their own.
- They are tired of bosses thinking they should be tied to their phone 24/7.

---

[4] Economy, "Millennials."

This generation has received an inaccurate reputation as lazy and entitled. There are lazy and entitled people in every generation. So why did this generation get all the negative press over the past decade? It's simple: they are not keeping their mouths shut. They are speaking out about how ridiculous it is to work 60 hours a week to only make ends meet and how high their student debt is. They started questioning all the things that my generation took as status quo because we were also taught very explicitly not to rock the boat.

Why do millennials think companies have it wrong?

- **Company culture:** They want a productive and positive culture with no discrimination. Positive culture is so much more than most businesses realize. It isn't just words and free food anymore.
- **Tolerating low performance:** They believe it is debilitating to see people get away with not doing the work that is assigned. Even worse, they see these people get promotions, raises, and bonuses.
- **Human Resources:** They believe Human Resources should be held accountable for making sure discrimination does not occur. Human Resources should be the employees' advocate.
- **Adult Bullies:** They don't want to work in an environment where people yell and scream at them. They don't believe whoever screams the loudest should win. In fact, they see that these Adult Bullies are being rewarded for their bad behavior and it needs to stop.
- **Get personal:** They want you to get to know them. They don't want to be treated like a number. They want to know about their manager as well.

- **Meaningless work:** They want to have a job. They just see all the meaningless work and want to find a better way. The countless hours spent on a PowerPoint presentation that will only be looked at for ten minutes is ludicrous in their minds. It should be preposterous to everyone.
- **Mentoring:** They need and crave mentoring They want to do a great job and be praised. But managers don't think they should help their employees. A manager shouldn't give an assignment, not help when asked for assistance, then throw a yelling fit when the job wasn't done exactly the way they wanted it.
- **High school:** They don't want to work in an organization that does not recognize and promote its employees. They see the cliques and the favoritism, and they think it is absurd. Why should employees have to kiss someone's ass for a promotion? Why can't the business do the right thing for the company and hire the most qualified person?
- **It's ok that it is just a job:** They are not defined by their work. All previous generations have defined their success by who they work for and what title they have. They want to have a good job, but do not define themselves by what they do. Work will not be their life. *We all should take this clue.*

Millennials are not going to allow these discriminatory and unproductive behaviors. In fact, companies are having to learn how to deal with their employees ghosting them. Employees don't feel the need to give their two weeks' notice, especially when they have been communicating the problems to management that is not listening. "I gave my bosses every opportunity to hear and understand what my concerns were and ample opportunity to act. If it's that low on their priority list, if there's that little urgency to resolve the issue that I'm bringing forward, then I don't have a f*cking ounce of respect for you. I don't have any desire to extend any kind of professional courtesy to you," stated Eric Samson in an article for Vice News.[5] This goes for Generation Z as well. They are no longer too shy to ask for what they expect for out of their jobs.

KRT Inaction—Millennial Bias Example

Swana graduated college and started to work at her dream job in retail. She was managing a big-box retail store that produced over $60M in sales the last year. She was brought in to help increase sales, but to also help change the culture of the store. The last manager was promoted to a different store.

Within the first week at the store, Henry, a department lead, told Swana straight to her face that he didn't respect her because she was too young and could never do the job that the last manager did. (It also didn't help she was a woman.) She accepted Henry's comment and told him that she was going to show him what a great leader she would be.

Henry wasn't happy with how she reacted because he wanted her gone. To him, she was an entitled millennial who had no idea what hard work was. Henry would complain to anyone who would listen. Most other employees ignored him, but a few did join his bandwagon.

In their first all-employee meeting, Swana shared her story of growing up poor and working two jobs in high school. She worked hard to make money to go to college and to get scholarships. She was the first person in her family to graduate from college and she was so excited to be working for this company for the past year. She was sure she was going to be the leader that they deserved.

---

[5]Gaviola, "Companies."

As you could have guessed, Henry's assumption was totally wrong about Swana. Within 30 minutes of the meeting, Henry went and apologized for jumping to the wrong conclusion.

KRT Recap

Henry was letting his unconscious bias get the better of him. If the KRT model was being used, he would have learned about Swana instead of jumping to a conclusion that was inaccurate.

Millennials were told they could be anything. Yes, they received trophies for just showing up, but what does that have to do with the reality of business? They have been taught that all people are equal and deserve a chance and respect. This is where the pivotal business change needs to occur. This paradigm shift is inevitable, and baby boomers/Gen X need to step up to the challenge if they want their companies to be successful.

Generation X is stuck in the middle between boomers and millennials and will never be the majority of anything with only 66 million. They are drenched in irony, detachment, and a sense of dread. Gen X has been used, abused, screamed at, and ignored for the better part of their lives. They have worked through more recessions than their parents or grandparents ever did. They were never given medals for participation and failure was how they learned.

Generation X is the most misunderstood generation because they have been ignored by the boomers, yet they are a company's intellectual capital. Companies' cultures have been defined by the boomers with Gen X following along—all while they don't feel valued. They are the last generation that is trying to stay at companies for the long haul. Gen X can see all the flaws from the past because they have been silently watching the corporations' greed.

Gen X must step up to help guide corporations and our government into the future. The command and control culture is dying, and the sooner corporations learn this lesson the better they will be poised for the future. Millennials are our future and it is time to open our eyes to the changes that need to be made.

As a society, our definition of what it means to have a job and work has shifted. We should be working so that we have free time for ourselves, family, and community. We shouldn't be working ourselves into the ground for low pay, long hours, and no health insurance. Even workers who are college educated are making working long hours normal and it is making them miserable.

"Millennials are often portrayed as apathetic, disinterested, tuned out, and selfish. None of those adjectives describe the Millennials I've been privileged to meet and work with."

—Chelsea Clinton
Global Health Advocate

MEDIA'S EFFECT ON ALL OF US

Look, we all know that media can be used for good or bad. But did you realize that very few companies control the majority of TV in the U.S.? In 1983, media was controlled by fifty different companies, now there are seven companies controlling the majority of information for approximately 329 million Americans. Does this make sense?

- AT&T—CNN, HBO (Cinemax), Turner (TNT, TBS, Cartoon Network, HLN, truTV), and Warner Bros (New Line Studios)
- CBS—CBS, CW, Showtime, Smithsonian, and Pop
- Comcast—NBC universal part of Hulu, MSNBC, Universal Pictures, E!, and Telemundo
- Disney—ABC, ESPN, Freeform, Lucasfilm, Pixar, Marvel Entertainment, FX, National Geographic, part of Hulu, Fox Movie Studio, and Fox TV studio
- Fox Corporation—Fox Broadcasting Network, Fox News, Fox Business Network, and Fox Sports Networks
- Netflix
- Viacom—MTV, Nickelodeon, BET, CMT, Comedy Central, VH1, and Paramount Pictures

Note: As of September 2019, CBS is wanting to purchase Viacom.

Confirmation Bias: The tendency to search for, interpret, favor, and recall information in a way that confirms one's preexisting beliefs of hypotheses

---

In 2018, AT&T purchased Time Warner to add to their entertainment portfolio. What they didn't talk about was the huge layoffs they would have. In 2019, the Fox deal was closed, with Disney taking over some assets and Fox Corp. separating from the movie and TV production business. What they said after the deal is that they would have huge layoffs to make the numbers work. In March 2019, Apple announced that they would also be starting their original content with Apple TV+, which will be creating brand-new jobs.

Why is this important?

In 1949, the Federal Communications Commission (FCC) introduced the Fairness Doctrine. This policy required holders of broadcast licenses to present controversial issues of public importance and to do so in a manner that was honest, equitable, and balanced. Under the Reagan administration, the FCC eliminated this policy in 1987. Right after this policy was removed is when Fox News, Rush Limbaugh, and other conservative media became much larger. Many experts believe that the removal of this policy is what has led to the rising level of political party polarization. Data has shown that people who only watch and listen to conservative media are more likely to believe and share fake news.[6] We have made being objective a political weapon.

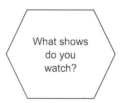

Confirmation bias is the tendency for people to embrace information that supports their beliefs and reject information that

---

[6]Hern, "Fake news."

contradicts them. Some people opt for propaganda over reality, while other people are more interested in the facts before ideology. People believe they know way more information than they actually do. They can be manipulated into believing almost anything if the news tells them it is true. Think of it as mass gaslighting that spins partial truths and dishonesties in order to manipulate information in ways that will help one side or the other win.

> **Cognitive Dissonance:** the mental discomfort (psychological stress) experienced by a person who holds two or more contradictory beliefs, ideas, or values

With confirmation bias, we embrace the information that confirms our beliefs. Then, when confronted with new information, we seek to preserve our current understanding. Our own cognitive dissonance is causing us to reject, explain away, or even avoid new information. We convince ourselves that there is no conflict. We don't like change and if we are faced with new information we may have to change. We like our comfortable lies and our status quo.

We are limiting our potential with our own actions. We all know science is real, yet 25% to 50% of our population doesn't believe climate change is real. The evidence is out there. But somewhere we were told it wasn't real, and now we will only read information that confirms it isn't real and reject anything that contradicts what we're told. We are accepting and promoting the lies as the truth.

Think about it this way, we all know that smoking is bad for your health. Yet smokers rationalize their smoking. I know I did. What if you were told that your grandmother smoked for most of her life and she did not have lung cancer when she died? You can see how a person can rationalize that smoking will not affect them.

Here is another example. Most of us believe we are smart about our online privacy, yet we take quizzes online or on the Facebook app. These quizzes ask a lot of personal information. Yet we freely give it away so that we can find out what superhero we would be or how smart we are. The information we give away in those quizzes can be data mined and sold to the highest bidder which, in turn, can use our information to continue to provide falsehoods and fake articles.

The fake articles have more readers than the real headlines. BuzzFeed News looked at 19 major news outlets, hoax sites, and hyper-partisan news.[7] During the last three months leading to the 2016 election, the top 20 fake articles were shared, liked, or commented on more than 8.7 million times while the top 20 real news stories had fewer than 7.4 million responses. We are being conditioned to react and not respond. We are not researching for the truth and are just reacting by sharing the fake news. This type of irrational reaction is what the person/group who put out the fake news intended. It's time we are better than this.

These fake news stories are causing problems across the board. People are getting gaslighted on a massive scale. On December 4, 2016, a fake news story that ran during the election caused a restaurant to be targeted. A man from North Carolina armed with an assault rifle decided to investigate Hillary Clinton for running a child sex ring out of a pizza place. He entered the restaurant with the rifle and one other gun. He fired the rifle but did not injure anyone.

In the 2000s, TV started new genres including the expansion of reality TV, the increased popularity of the anti-hero, and many more crime shows. We were watching shows like *The Sopranos* and

---

[7]Silverman, "Analysis."

Dexter, where we started rooting for the mob boss and a killer. We were watching *Survivor* and *The Apprentice*, where we cheered as people were being belittled and made to feel worthless.

We were living in a post-9/11 world where fear was our normal. Technology was catching up and we now had DVRs and then Netflix. We started binge watching shows. We needed to escape from the reality that our world was never going to be the same. People were now able to watch programming on demand and were not missing the shows they wanted to see.

Fast-forward another decade and we now have many streaming services such as Hulu and Amazon Prime. You can access billions of videos on YouTube. You can access media anywhere on a smart device. We have become accustomed to instant gratification with our media. What type of programming are they making for us now?

Here is breakdown of programming on the four major networks (ABC, CBS, Fox, and NBC) and CW.

2016 vs. 2018:

Type of Show	Fall 2016 %	Spring 2018 %
Crime/Drama	48.00%	36.11%
Comedy	21.33%	27.78%
Reality	18.67%	27.78%
Fantasy	12.00%	8.33%

What we are watching:

- 36–48% of programming is Crime/Drama
- 60% of Top 10 shows are Crime/Drama

- Included in these shows are:
  - violence and death
  - discrimination
  - racism
  - misogyny and sexism
  - sexual harassment or assault
  - examples of hostile work environments being normal
  - women backstabbing women (fighting over men)
  - corruption (government, police, business)
  - Adult Bullies and gaslighting

What have you learned from watching TV and movies? What lessons are they teaching us? People learn from what they see and, if what they see is bad behaviors, can we blame them for thinking that so much violence, discrimination, and misconduct toward women and other races is normal?

There have been many studies around how media violence affects the brain. Here are some findings:[8,9]

- National Institute of Mental Health—1982 report
  - Children may become less sensitive to the pain and suffering of others.
  - Children may be more fearful of the world around them.
  - Children may be more likely to behave in aggressive and harmful ways toward others.
- Virginia Tech Research Division
  - Violent films can increase hostile behavior.

[8]Anderson and Warburton, "Violent video games."
[9]Archer, "Violence."

- University of Alabama
  - ○ Aggressive behavior continues after viewing a violent film.
- Macquarie University
  - ○ Children who watch violent movies are more likely to the view the world as an unsympathetic, malicious, and scary place. Children are more likely to exhibit combative behavior while becoming desensitized to violence.

Society is opening its eyes to the truth and we do not like what we are seeing. Shows such as *Supergirl* and *The Good Place* are breaking this mold and trying to teach positive values. But these shows aren't always sustaining the viewers that the networks need to make their money. *Heartbeat, Conviction*, and *Good Girls Revolt* were canceled after just one season. *Supergirl* was relocated to the CW, because CBS wasn't making the money they wanted. The positive shows don't make as much money as the crime-based, violence-based shows. What does that say about us as a country?

Why do we like watching reality TV? We know reality TV is not reality. Or do we? What reality TV does do is show us the worst qualities in people, including the constant anger and fighting. Does popular culture have any values left or are we just concerned with greed and success? Reality TV is cheap to produce and has proven to be a money maker for its creators.

Marketing is quite smart. It makes us believe we are deficient in something. This technique is used to keep us coming back for more. Reality TV are shows that are based on drama and narcissism. These shows are intensifying people's dreams of fame and how life should be. They want to be like their idols on TV. They want to use the products and have the same clothes. Do you ever wonder how much these celebrities are getting paid for their endorsements of a product they are telling you to buy?

Let's take a specific look at the reality show called *The Bachelor*. Within this show you will see what women will do to get the affection of a man. I honestly can say I never concerned myself with this show, but it has a huge viewer base. So, why do we watch women being demeaned, dehumanized, and publicly humiliated? Why do these women want to compete for the affection of man?

The Bachelor—Reality TV example (dating game)

- 23rd season aired in Spring 2019.
- Women are shown to be desperate to find love.
- Very little diversity—mostly white women.
- Women fight with other women to gain the affection of the bachelor.
- When the woman is not worthy of the bachelor, he does not give the women a rose. This is public humiliation.
- The bachelor will kiss and make out with as many women as he wants. He is never shamed for doing this.
- When a woman makes out with the bachelor, she will be called a name by the other women for making out with him.
- The bachelor controls the women by holding over their heads the reward of a one-on-one date.
- The bachelor has all the power and only the woman who the bachelor wants is worthy of his love.

There are articles that say *The Bachelor* is a guilty pleasure and that the women watching the show use it to escape from their own lives/romances. Why do women really like watching the competition between women for love? Are our lives so bad that we want misery and heartbreak for other people? Does this show change how you handle your own relationships?

Of course, I know that there is also *The Bachelorette* show that makes men compete over a woman. I have the same thoughts on that show as well. Why do we want to compete for someone to love us? I know the women and men on these shows are doing it for the fame and maybe love, but is it worth it?

TV has helped socialize us from a young age to assign people into different categories. We see the cool kids (jocks/cheerleaders) versus the uncool kids (nerds/artists). We see society—including our schoolteachers and parents—adding labels to everything we do or who we are. These labels are for one reason and one reason only: to show the superiority of one group over the other.

Growing up in the 1980s and 1990s, both TV and movies were littered with bad behaviors that we were taught were ok. Remember the movie the *Revenge of the Nerds*? We were taught it was ok to rape women. The nerd deceived the girl by wearing a costume and had sex with her. She had thought it was a different man. This same scenario happened in the movie *Sixteen Candles*. The girl had sex with the nerd but thought it had been her boyfriend. Why was this ever thought to be ok? This is called rape by deception. These movies perpetuated the basic idea that even though both women had been raped, it was ok because it all worked out in the end with the girls choosing their rapist as their new boyfriend.

These movies taught girls and women that if they get drunk, they were asking for it. That boys and men will help their friend get the girl even if she is passed out because consent doesn't matter. The kind of girl who gets raped cannot complain because she was asking for it by drinking or wearing clothing that turned on the man. The good guy can participate in the rape and remain the good guy who the girl wants to date.

These issues only got worse as I grew up watching *21 Jump Street*; *Beverly Hills, 90210*; and MTV. I remember watching Kelly and Brenda fight over Dylan. Dylan had cheated on Brenda with Kelly. Kelly was Brenda's best friend. In the end, the women decided to let the man choose who he wanted to be with. These two women just handed the man (who didn't respect either one because he cheated) the keys to choose who he wanted to date. WTF was I watching?

Did the media realize they were:

- Teaching young girls to fight over boys who don't respect them.
- Teaching young girls to not trust other girls (Don't respect your best friend.)
- Showing girls that boys are more important than female friendship.
- Showing girls that boys have all the power.

Yes, the media and marketing know exactly what they are doing. Fast-forward to the show *Sex and the City*. We watched Carrie Bradshaw chase after a man who treated her with constant disrespect. We watched the normalization of abusive behavior when one of Carrie's friend goes back to her toxic marriage with a man because she doesn't want to be alone.

What about *The Secret Life of the American Teenager*? This show made sure to keep stereotypes and sexist behaviors normalized. The life lesson was that the girl should keep her legs closed or she will get pregnant with no blame or shame for the boy who impregnated her. The dad yelled at his girls about sex and the girls were shamed for showing their bodies. Don't forget about the sexist jokes about breasts and weight.

This all leads back to the command and control (strict father morality) culture we have been living in. We don't even realize how the media affects our behaviors and beliefs. Media uses many different psychology tricks to get you to buy into what they are selling. Are they priming you, using a decoy, making you think there is scarcity (when there is none), or even giving you false stories to create their narrative? Remember shows on TV are trying to sell you on something whether it is a product or an idea.

Think about it this way, the primary source of information in the 1980s and 1990s was your TV. Every household had a TV and most even had cable TV. This new source of information was run by mostly—if not all—men. Men controlled what women watched. This has led to the increased objectification of women while teaching them to be subservient. This plays out in other forms of media as well.

Sexism: Discrimination based on gender, especially women

Do men's magazines objectify women and celebrate excessive masculinity? You bet they do. These magazines normalize the sexism and misogyny among their readers. They write about bad behaviors like locker room talk as normal and that sexist jokes are ok. This is another piece of the sexism puzzle that must change to help our future.

Let's think about this in relationship to the news. Does negative news affect you? Yes. It directly affects your mood which, in turn, affects other parts of your life. News networks can manipulate facts to promote their agenda (Right, neutral, and Left).

They are using negative words to make you feel fearful and make fun of or degrade anyone who does not believe exactly as they do. How many times have you heard a newscaster make up a name for someone they didn't like? Negative news makes you feel like everything is bad, especially when all you see is constant negativity. If you are watching the same news show day after day, then you may not realize what tactics they are using to keep you coming back. It is important to be diverse in your news so that you can see the whole picture.

"Whoever controls the media, controls the mind."

—Jim Morrison
Songwriter/Musician

PAY/INCOME GAP

I was part of Corporate America for more than half of my career. During that time, I was told by my management and Human Resources that I should not discuss salary (even when I heard men talking in the hallway about theirs). I was told not to worry that pay grades (pay scale) are fair (yet I saw many men get promoted to the same job and make more money than a woman/person of color who had been in the job for a few years). This is how Corporate America works. If you talk to your management or Human Resource about the salary differences, they try to gaslight you into believing you heard wrong so that you will stop asking questions. Or they harass or threaten you by telling you to quit and find a new job because you are overreacting. This happens daily.

How do pay/income gaps continue to occur?

- Sexism/Misogyny
- Racism
- Salary audits are nonexistent or not public
- Management and Human Resources tell you not to talk about your salary
- Large pay grades (pay scale) for each title (some $50,000 to $75,000)
- Bonuses are not equally distributed

Pay Audit: A pay audit involves comparing the pay of all people doing equal work in your organization. An audit is not simply a data collection exercise. It entails a commitment to put right any unfair pay inequalities.

There is hope on the horizon. The state of Oregon has created their own Equal Pay Act (EPA) for 2017. They are trying to lead the way for all corporations to fix this issue themselves. The question is, will big corporations step up to the plate and fix the problem? The answer: not without employees taking a stand.

To be effective, it will take all employees taking a stand. People are so busy making ends meet by trying to "Keep up with the Kardashians" they may not even know there is a problem. Or they believe that there cannot be a problem because there is a law for that. Due to the misinformation in the media, education and knowledge are needed to help employees see that there really are issues. We need changes in businesses, but also in our legislation at local, state, and national levels.

Effective in 2018, companies in Iceland are now required to demonstrate they pay men and women fairly. This new law applies to both private and public jobs. In 1963, Iceland mandated equal pay for equal work. Now in 2018, it is up to the companies—not the employee—to prove that their pay practices are fair. This new law applies to companies with 25+ employees. Every three years they must be certified that they are paying equally. This new law passed a year after female candidates won nearly half the seats in Iceland's Parliament.

In the U.S., we are not proactive and businesses have *willingly and knowingly* allowed the pay gap to continue. Businesses are not required to prove they are following the law. It is up to the individual to report the issue so that it can be investigated. Why, if the U.S. has a law on equal pay, is it so hard to actually pay people the same?

Learn more about Pay Audits at
www.bekindtoall.com/payaudit

People have been led to believe that if women, LGBTQ+, and people of color get a fair share, their percentage of the pie will change. That is 100% false. In reality, everyone's piece of the pie grows as the wealth stops flowing almost exclusively to the top 1%. This money could help us to start to close the income inequality gap.

Should women continue to keep their mouths shut? This is what corporations and Human Resources want. If we start talking to each other, we will find the truth. Just like the young lady who found out her male friend got offered more money for the same job at a Pizza Studio restaurant. When she questioned the issue, the company withdrew both job offers. The U.S. Equal Employment Opportunity Commission (EEOC) is now suing the company for violations of the Equal Pay Act.[10]

On January 4, 2017, the Department of Labor filed a lawsuit to require Google to provide requested compensation data due to "systemic compensation disparities." They had found disparities against women throughout their workforce. On September 14, 2017, a class action lawsuit was filed against Google due to their practices of systematically paying women less by segregating women into lower-paying jobs and stifling their careers.[11]

Your employer is breaking the law if they tell you that you cannot discuss your salary. The National Labor Relations Act of 1935 (NLRA) states that all workers have the right to engage "concerted activity for mutual aid or protection" and "organize a union to negotiate with employer concerning wages, hours and other terms and conditions of employment." Yet, Human Resources tell employees every day to not discuss their salaries. This law is for everyone from line workers to management. This type of pay secrecy is how companies keep their employees in line and keep their command and control culture.

The Paycheck Fairness Act was proposed legislation that would add procedural protections to the Equal Pay Act of 1963 and the Fair Labor Standards Act as part of an effort to address male-female income disparity in the U.S. Republican lawmakers have blocked this act because they don't want the employers to have increased lawsuits. Seriously, the U.S. has blocked equal pay for equal work because they don't want employers to have

[10]Viviani, "EEOC."

[11]Levin, "Google."

to show how they discriminate. This type of behavior is far more concerning than we have given it credit for.

Companies treat employees with surveillance and regulations that some would say even violates our constitutional rights. American workers have very few rights when it comes to their employment and even how their bosses treat them. Companies may have a code of business conduct, but in most companies, these policies are weakly enforced—if at all. Although workers are free to leave their jobs, with nearly one-fifth of all workers under non-compete clauses, if they quit or are fired, they cannot work in the same industry. This holds employees hostage in their jobs.

At Salesforce, their CEO Marc Benioff is dedicated to closing the gender pay gap. This company is so dedicated to remove the pay gap; they have conducted two assessments (2015/2017) to find out if they need to adjust pay. They found both times they needed to spend $3 million to eliminate these differences in pay. Looking into the future, they will continue to monitor future pay gaps.[12] Imagine if your company was proactive like that? Why haven't we demanded this of companies we work for?

Even the courts cannot make up their mind on the equal pay issue:[13,14,15]

- In 2015, there was a ruling that stated basing women's salaries on their prior salaries was inherently discriminatory, since they likely faced pay discrimination due to gender bias at their former jobs.

[12]Brinded, "Benioff."

[13]Hatch, "Federal Court."

[14]Paquette, "Employers."

[15]Campbell, "9th Circuit."

- On April 27, 2017, a three-judge panel of the Ninth Circuit Court of Appeals of California ruled to overturn a 2015 ruling. With this new ruling that is no longer the case. They cited a 1982 ruling by the court that said employers could use previous salary information as long as they applied it reasonably and had a business policy that justified it.

- Then, on April 9, 2018, an 11-judge panel for the Ninth Circuit Court of Appeals overturned the ruling from 2017. Employers cannot use a woman's salary history to rationalize paying them less than a man doing the same job.

"Although the Act has prohibited sex-based wage discrimination for more than fifty years, the financial exploitation of working women embodied by the gender pay gap continues to be an embarrassing reality of our economy."

—Circuit Judge Stephen Reinhardt
Ninth Circuit Court of Appeals Judge

Human Resources allows discriminations in all its forms to continue. Why do you think black Americans make 74% of what white males make and women make 77% to 90% of what white males make? *It is simple: Human Resources allows it.* If you have been in this circumstance and you report it to Human Resources, they will most likely do nothing. They tell you to talk to your manager. Then your manager tells you that it isn't in the budget. EEOC will consider these claims, but the company's Human Resources makes sure to cover the company and most likely nothing is ever done.

You only have
six months after
you quit to make
any allegations to
the EEOC.

President Obama had worked with the EEOC to develop regulations to address these pay disparities. This new regulation was set to collect its first batch of data in March 2018. On August 29, 2017, under the Trump Administration, the EEOC published a memo that stated it would freeze the rule voicing concerns that gathering pay information would place an outsize burden on the employers for little benefit. This should sound familiar because this is what happened with the Paycheck Fairness Act.

Did you know that there is an Equal Pay Day each year? Equal Pay Day is April 10 and it has been happening for 23 years since 1996. At the current pace of pay equality, it will be at least 100 years. *This is not acceptable.*

80% of women
would leave a
company for one
that offered better
gender equality.

It is time for **radical transparency**. It is time to be **brave** and discuss pay gaps. If we remain silent nothing will change. *Keeping our mouths shut is how we got here. It is time for a new approach.*

KRT In Action:
- Ask your Human Resources/Management:
  - For an independent public salary audit to prove that all women, LGBTQ+, and people of color are being paid the same wage for the same work.
  - For a public document that shows how many women, LGBTQ+, and people of color are in the different positions within the company.
  - To investigate and publish how gender bias, racism, and sexism affects yearly evaluations for women, LGBTQ+, and people of color.
  - Stand up and talk about your salary/bonus/rating with your peers.

This change will be good for every company, our country, our economy, and our equality.

Latest Pay Gap data:
https://www.glassdoor.com/research/
studies/gender-pay-gap-2019/

INCOME INEQUALITY

Income inequality is the unequal distribution of household or individual income across the various participants in an economy. Income inequality is often presented as the percentage of income to a percentage of population.

History shows us that change is slow but will occur. The United Nations shows us that the U.S. is lagging far behind international human rights standards. Let that sink in for a moment. The U.S. is lagging **far** behind international human rights standards. The U.S. has a lot of work to do and it's time we stop skirting the issue. America's poor are becoming more destitute each year. Poverty is widespread and is deepening because of the removal of the safety nets that were in place.

The War on Poverty was introduced by President Johnson in 1964. Johnson believed that expanding the federal government's roles in education and healthcare would work as poverty reduction strategies. He believed that we must cure and prevent poverty. The popularity of this idea dwindled after the 1960s. This is not a political issue because both sides of the aisle have allowed and created these income gaps.

Right now, in the U.S., we have more than 40 million people who live in poverty. At the population size of approximately 329 million, that means more than 12% of all Americans live in poverty—including many of our veterans. This number includes 18.5 million in extreme poverty with more than six million children. This is not getting better; this is getting worse. The safety nets that were put into place are being removed slowly. This is happening at an increasing pace under the 45th president with his harm the poor while giving tax breaks to the rich agenda. Poverty is not a human failure. 80% of all wealth is inherited. Did you know during the 1950s and early 1960s, the top bracket income tax rate was over 90%? Can you guess what happened? The economy, middle-class, and stock market boomed.

> *"In 1980, there were a few hundred emergency food programs across the country; today there are 50,000. One in six people report running out of food at least once per year. In many European countries by contrast, the number is closer to one in twenty."*
>
> **—Tracie McMillion**
> "The New Face of Hunger," *National Geographic*

We cannot overcome what we ignore. Keeping people poor and unhealthy makes sure that they don't have the time to worry about their government or community. They don't have time to get a better education because they have to work all the time. It is time that we create policies to help all Americans, especially people in poverty.

Did you know that President Franklin D. Roosevelt created and named a Second Bill of Rights in his State of the Union Address on January 11, 1944? Roosevelt suggested that the nation had come to recognize and should now implement, a second Bill of Rights. Roosevelt's argument was that the "political rights" guaranteed by the U.S. Constitution and the Bill of Rights had "proved inadequate to assure us equality in the pursuit of happiness." His remedy was to declare an "economic bill of rights" to guarantee these specific rights. Here is an excerpt of his speech:[16]

We have come to a clear realization of the fact that true individual freedom cannot exist without economic security and independence. "Necessitous men are not free men." People who are hungry and out of a job are the stuff of which dictatorships are made.

---

[16]Wikipedia, "Second Bill of Rights."

In our day these economic truths have become accepted as self-evident. We have accepted, so to speak, a second Bill of Rights under which a new basis of security and prosperity can be established for all—regardless of station, race, or creed.

Among these are:

- *The right to a useful and remunerative job in the industries or shops or farms or mines of the nation;*
- *The right to earn enough to provide adequate food and clothing and recreation;*
- *The right of every farmer to raise and sell his products at a return which will give him and his family a decent living;*
- *The right of every businessman, large and small, to trade in an atmosphere of freedom from unfair competition and domination by monopolies at home or abroad;*
- *The right of every family to a decent home;*
- *The right to adequate medical care and the opportunity to achieve and enjoy good health;*
- *The right to adequate protection from the economic fears of old age, sickness, accident, and unemployment;*
- *The right to a good education.*

Roosevelt died before he was able to implement the Second Bill of Rights for the workers. Imagine if he had succeeded how different our world would be. We would not have the rampant discrimination and greed that is running large businesses today. We would take care of our fellow Americans: healthcare, education, and a livable wage would be rights not privileges.

During this century, Occupy Wall Street brought visibility to America's glaring income gap. But this income gap has not been collapsing, it has continued to widen. In the article "The Oligarchy Economy: Concentrated Power, Income Inequality, and Slow Growth," Jordan Brennan explains how corporate concentration exacerbates income inequality.[17] On the other side, trade union power helps alleviate the inequality. Unions have been declining in part because of capitalism and free enterprise system since the early 1980s. Companies have been focusing on mergers and acquisitions as well as repurchasing their own stock. They have forgotten what financial integrity means for their employees. They started caring about the bottom line not the employees. Greed over people.

This is evidenced by years and years of acquisitions and surpluses. I went through 15 years straight of surpluses at a Fortune 10 company. Seriously, 15 years of worrying if I was going to be laid off or if I was going to have to surplus my team. Since I have left, they have continued their streak. The insidious part of all of this is how Human Resources handles each department differently. This will be covered later in Chapter 2.

Capitalism has allowed our world to create and build the most amazing things. But most big businesses have stopped caring about their employees and only care about their bottom line. By focusing only on money, companies have been causing themselves unnecessary employee turnover, talent loss, and unproductivity. Most companies have decided that employees are dispensable and easily replaceable. But did anyone step up and say that saving existing employees makes more sense for our bottom line? Being a big business shouldn't mean that you can treat people any way you want. We have accepted certain aspects of our lives to be normal

---

[17]Brennan, "Oligarchy."

that really should not be. Why do we prioritize money over basic things like our environment, water, and communities? Why do we think of love and compassion as a weakness?

We started the 21st century with the Enron and Arthur Andersen scandals. Enron had been named America's Most Innovative Company for six years straight. They claimed $101 billion in revenue in 2000. Then, at the end of 2001, we learned about their corporate accounting fraud. Thanks to this scandal, we enacted the Sarbanes-Oxley Act of 2002. But this didn't help the tens of thousands of employees who lost their jobs and retirement due to the greed of a few men at top.

Let's not forget how Wall Street and the government lied to the public repeatedly before the 2008 stock market crash on September 28. The signs were there for all of us to see. Bear Stearns was bailed out by the Feds in March 2008 to try to save the company. Now remember, this company was heavily involved in the subprime mortgage crisis that occurred. In the end, the company could not be saved and was sold to JPMorgan Chase & Co.

The financial crisis of 2008 came to a head on September 15 when Lehman Brothers went bankrupt. Their excessive risk-taking helped lead us to the most serious financial crisis since the Great Depression. On September 17, the government gave AIG $85 billion to help stabilize the market, but it didn't help even though the Federal Reserve took over AIG. On September 8, the bull market failed and dropped almost 800 points. In response, the government passed the Emergency Economic Stabilization Act of 2008, which gave $700 billion into the Troubled Asset Relief Program (TARP) to help recover the market. The Dodd-Frank Wall Street Reform and Consumer Protection Act, which was signed into law in 2010, reduced the amount authorized to $475 billion.

In 2012, the Congressional Budget Office (CBO) stated the total would be around $431 billion.

The TARP was just one piece of the recovery that the government helped with. They also created the American Recovery and Reinvestment Act of 2009 (ARRA), which was a stimulus package to help save existing jobs with a price tag of $787 billion, which was increased to $831 billion. This act helped by extending unemployment benefits and providing money for infrastructure and more money to education.

While our tax dollars (which were never paid back from these businesses) were bailing out the "too big to fail" entities, millions of people were in complete devastation with layoffs up to 750,000 each month. During this crisis, the CEOs of the banks (who got the bailout) still received their bonuses. For example, AIG paid more than $1 million each to 73 employees of AIG Financial Products. Fannie Mae and Freddie Mac paid out more than $200 million in bonuses between 2008 and 2010, even though the firms lost more than $100 billion in 2008 alone and required nearly $400 billion in federal assistance during the bailout period. Why would any company think they should do this? They were capitalizing on other people's misfortunes and their own bad decisions.

Let's take a minute and look at Bernie Madoff and how his Ponzi scheme came tumbling down. The financial crisis not only exposed the problems with mortgage lending, it exposed other bad behaviors and bad business practices. Bernie Madoff Investment Securities LLC had an estimated fraud worth approximately $65 billion. This Ponzi scheme had started back in the 1980s and 1990s and came tumbling down because of the stock crash of 2008. Bernie had given sizeable donations to political candidates, parties, and committees, which gave him access to our government that a "normal" person would not have. This helped him when his name first came up for fraud investigation in the 1990s. In the end, Bernie was sentenced to 150 years in jail for 11 federal felonies.

Greed: A selfish desire to have more of something (especially money)

Did you ever wonder why people fight so hard on Black Friday to get the cheapest products? Companies have been training us for decades now to fight for the lowest priced item. They have been pitting us against each other to see who can win by grabbing that discounted TV. But why? To keep us blinded to their greed. They aren't doing these sales for us. They are doing these sales to make more money for themselves. They have trained us, like sheep, to go and wait in line for the discounts. Aren't you tired of competing for low prices that really aren't that low when you dig into it? This is how greed operates in our economy.

Another interesting part of greed is how it discriminates against women. Have you heard of the Pink Tax? It's gender-based pricing discrimination. Women are charged more for the same product. For example, women's razors cost up to 10% more than their male counterparts. Women pay more for products and services and when combined with the pay gap and added to the fact that women are taxed on their feminine hygiene products, women have less buying power.

Let's talk about the business of disease. The healthcare industry, which includes the drug companies, are not fighting to lower prices. They are fighting to make more money by treating the symptom instead of the whole person. Did you know that the U.S.

is one of only two countries in the entire world that allows drugs to be advertised directly to the consumer? We didn't allow this until 1985. What do other countries pay for the same drug? For example, in 2015, Xarelto (used to treat blood clots) cost on average $292 for a 30-day supply. But in the UK, it's $126, in Switzerland it is $102, and in South Africa just $48.

Did you know that Medicare (which my parents are on) is not a low-cost provider for prescriptions? In 2017, my mom and I both had to go on Tamiflu. My mom on Medicare paid $149.99, while my co pay was just $20. But that isn't what my mother paid, because we knew about GoodRX. We used the GoodRX app to get my mom's prescription down to only $50, which was still 250% more than what I paid. Can you see the ridiculousness of all of this? You have insurance that you have paid into all your life, which charges you more for prescriptions than if you didn't have insurance. Everyone can use GoodRX and I would recommend downloading and looking at your own prescriptions.

Most drugs developed to cure diseases are being funded by our tax dollars. Yes, your money and mine is going to the research.[18] The research is being conducted by the big pharma companies. Once they have a breakthrough and have a new drug, they get to patent it and sell it for profit. They get to hold that patent for 20 years before a generic version can come out (if they choose to do so). Our money is paying for the development of these drugs.

Healthcare lobbyists (many are ex-congressmen and senators) have spent over $3.9 billion lobbying the U.S. Congress from 1998 to 2018. That is over $7,000,000 spent per member (total 535 – 100 Senators and 435 Congress). This is the big money in politics

---

[18]Cleary et al., "NIH."

that has been controlling our healthcare. Why is this considered normal?

Remember the polio vaccine that saved us? It was free. Why? To save lives. It was a simple philosophy. Yet today, we let people die every day because lifesaving drugs are too expensive for them to afford. If you can afford the cost, you may be causing yourself to go far in debt. An estimated 20% to 50% of all bankruptcies are due to healthcare expenses.

To recap:[19,20]

1. We (U.S. taxpayers) are funding these companies to develop the drugs to help us with our tax dollars.
2. The company gets a 20-year patent and sells the drug for a profit.
3. Consumers are given many different prices for the same drug based on their insurance and what they know. (Did they know about Good RX?)
4. The company spends their profits to lobby your congressman and senators with your ex congressmen/senators who went to work for the company after they served in government.[21] This is all so that they can keep this vicious greed cycle going
5. People are dying and/or going into debt just to stay alive.

Isn't it evil for us to let someone die when there is a way to save them?

---

[19]Mervis, "Data."
[20]Zaitchik, "Taxpayers."
[21]Frankenfield, "Lobbying."

Why do we think it is normal to go into extreme debt to keep our lives?

Looking at the latest scandals (Wells Fargo, EpiPen), we are seeing that greed is going unchecked. Greed is not how to run a business because you will get caught—or at least eventually you will get caught. Why not spend that money on equal wages for everyone?

KRT Inaction—Greed Example

Rad has worked for a grocery store for over three years. He is a food preparer and helps fulfill customers' orders. Rad is a very hard worker and has a good relationship with his management. Rad forgot to fill out his yearly appraisal form. He didn't realize he had not done this. Rad was almost six months late filling out his yearly appraisal form.

The employee manual states that a yearly review will be held with all employees. It also states it is the store leader's job to make sure that this discussion is taking place. Rad's manager never reminded him or even tried to have a yearly discussion until he turned in his form.

Rad's store leader did not follow procedure

Rad received his yearly raise six months late

Rad did not receive back pay

KRT Recap

There is no excuse for this blatant violation of the employee manual. Rad's manager never made an attempt to do the right thing. If the KRT model was being used, this manager would have reminded Rad about his appraisal when it was due, then made sure that he received his raise on time.

> How many employees has this business short-changed?

This is a great example of management placing the responsibility on the employee to get their yearly raise. Why would any business do this to their employees? Shouldn't the business know the employee's employment date and be proactive like the employee manual states? They should, but it's a cheap way to make a buck.

Indeed.com did a survey to find out how employees feel about their pay. Only 19% of employees are comfortable with their rate of pay. More men (54%) than women (41%) will be asking for pay raises this year. 68% of workers would consider additional benefits as an alternative to pay raises. Employees know they are underpaid but are willing to compromise.[22]

Work used to have dignity. America was the land of opportunity and fair play. In the 1970s, we traded the thought of "We all do better when we all do better" for "Greed is good." The data shows that around the middle 1970s is when income inequality started to widen again. This is when companies started paying more attention to productivity and how much they could get out of their workers.

---

[22]Indeed, "Report."

KRT Inaction—Productivity Gains Example

Lola was a reporting analyst. She had been doing this job for around five years. She was always busy and worked hard to make sure all of her reports were done on time. She had two counterparts who also worked on reports. Then, one day, one of these reporting analysts quit. At that point, Lola's job changed significantly.

Instead of replacing the analyst, her company decided that the work could now be done by just two people. Management claimed that with all the advances in reporting systems, this should be no problem. Management didn't understand the systems but felt certain it could be done. These two analysts now were working 60-hour weeks to get the work accomplished.

Within one year, Lola decided since they weren't going to pay her more money or get any help, she was going to leave the job. After Lola left, the company decided that the job could be done by one person. The one analyst who was left started working six days a week 12 hours per day to get the work done.

KRT Recap

Lola's management had decided on job changes without asking the person doing the work. Lola's manager did not listen or care that employees were working 60 hours a week. If the KRT model was being used, management would have asked Lola about the amount of work and time needed to do the reporting. They would have never forced 60-hour work weeks on her and her coworker.

This example shows exactly how workers have been treated. They are not getting their share of gains of productivity. In fact, employee productivity has skyrocketed by 21.6% from 2000 to 2014 yet wages only grew at 1.8%. Companies would rather have their employees do two to three people's job at the same pay as one person. This type of productivity enhancement benefits the upper management and not the employee.

Instead of sharing in the wealth (record breaking profits) of the company with these hardworking employees, the income is going to the already wealthy. It is time for companies to start sharing the wealth that their workers are creating. Companies should not be run just for the 1% to make more money.

If I hear the adages "pull yourself up by your bootstraps" and "it's your fault if you don't make a good wage," I just stare at the person saying them. That is truly not case in most instances. Employees are working many jobs and are still not able to afford necessities such as food and shelter. As a society, we have allowed these monopolies to control our lives by our paychecks. Unless we do something to knock down the barriers, average Americans won't have a chance. The average American is not gaining wealth, while the top 1%'s wealth is increasing at staggering rates. In fact, the richest 1% now owns more wealth than any time in the past 50 years.

Here are the disturbing facts of where we are:

Top 20% of U.S. households own more than 86% of all wealth

Top 1% average income is $1,363,977

Bottom 40% of U.S. households only have 0.3% of all wealth

Bottom 90% of Americans are poorer than they were in 2007 with an average income of $34,074

The Walton Family (Walmart) has more wealth than 42% of American families combined

In 2017, the 1% grabbed 82% of all wealth created

If all net worth (wealth) was divided among 124 million U.S. households that would be over $750,000 per family

Bottom 50% of families (62 million) average $11,000 net worth

Average worker must work one month to make what a CEO makes in one hour

78% of all Americans are living paycheck to paycheck, while most are in debt

Let's think about our income inequality in terms of a pizza: There are ten slices of pizza and there are ten people to share the slices of pizza. One person takes eight slices of pizza. That will leave two slices of pizza for the other nine people. Yes, this is how bad our income inequality is. Some statistics would even show there is only one slice left for the nine people. This is the truth of where we are.

Per Statistica, here is the breakdown in Household Income for 2017[23]:

$$	%	%
Under 15,000	10.7%	40.8%
15,000-24,999	9.6%	
25,000-34,999	8.2%	
35,000-49,999	12.3%	
50,000-74,999	16.5%	29.0%
75,000-99,999	12.5%	
100,000-149,999	14.5%	21.5%
150,000-199,999	7.0%	
Over 200,000	7.7%	7.7%

[23]Duffin, "Household income."

- 40.8% of all households make less than $50,000
- 69.8 % of all households make less than $100,000

Do these statistics surprise you? When I started researching income inequality, I had no idea that we had this large of a gap. Let's take this a step further.

Pay and Rent Cost Statistics:[24,25]
CEO pay has increased by over 600%

- 1985—46× the typical worker
- 2015—up to 300× the typical worker

While minimum wage has only increased by 216%

- 1985—minimum wage = $3.35
- 2018—minimum wage = $7.25

How does that affect an average worker with one full-time job?

	Monthly	Yearly
Minimum wage (40 hours)	$1,256.67 (pre-tax)	$15,080 (pre-tax)
Average rent (one bedroom)	$932.45	$11,189.40
Difference	$324.22	$3,890.60

That leaves only $324.22 a month to pay for:

- Taxes
- Health insurance

---
[24]Payscale, "CEOs."
[25]Donnelly, "CEOs."

- Health expenses
- Food
- Utilities
- Car payment
- Car insurance
- Cell phone
- Personal items (such as tampons)

How does making minimum wage compare to Federal Poverty Guidelines?[26]

- If there is more than one person in the household and the earner makes the federal minimum wage, they are **below** the Federal Poverty Guidelines.

# in household	Poverty Guideline (2018)	Minimum Wage (7.25)	Difference
1	$12,140	$15,080	$2,940
2	$16,460	$15,080	($1,380)
3	$20,780	$15,080	($5,700)
4	$25,100	$15,080	($10,020)

Are you thinking that most people don't make minimum wage? Yes, there is a push for increased wages, and in many states. In fact, 29 states have raised the minimum wage including Washington, D.C. at $12.50 per hour. In Florida, for example, the minimum wage is $8.46, and some places start at over $10 an hour.

The U.S. has one of the lowest minimum wage policies of any wealthy nation. In the past 27 years, the federal minimum wage has only increased by $3. Many states have raised their own

---

[26]U.S. Department of Health and Human Services, "Poverty."

minimum wage. The inaction of the federal government has led the states to fight for their employees. If wages kept up with productivity, the federal minimum wage would be worth about $19 an hour.

Instead of paying livable wages, we see the wealth concentrated in the hands of a few. The last time this happened was the Gilded Age (1870s to the early 1900s). Two acts were passed to help combat these issues. The Sherman Antitrust Act of 1890 which was ineffective, so in 1914 the Clayton Antitrust Act was passed. We are at the beginning of a new era. *We can live in an equitable society where people don't struggle for their basic needs.*

A new trend has been happening because of the low unemployment rate: companies are now paying lower wages if you can only work part time. For example, if you can work full time, you will start at $11 an hour for a total of $440 a week for full time. At the same company, they are paying $10.50 an hour if you can only work part time. This could be an interesting practice going forward, especially when the jobs are for younger people just joining the workforce. Or is this just another form of greed?

Real wages for jobs requiring a high school diploma and college degree have been dropping. For a person with a high school diploma, inflation adjusted wages have dropped by about 30% since 1970. For a person with a bachelor's degree, they have dropped 15%. All of this while the cost of a bachelor's degree has been increasing around 6.2% per year.

Cost of a bachelor's degree:
1970—$5,000
2017—$80,000

When we dig into an apples-to-apples comparison using 2013 dollars and removing inflation, we can easily see how real wages are not keeping up. In 1970, a person with a high school diploma would be earning $37,000 (in 2013 dollars) and a person with a bachelor's degree would be earning $53,000 (in 2013 dollars). The degree would cost about $30,000 (in 2013 dollars). This equates to a bachelor's degree costing you about half a years' worth of salary. Today a person makes around $25,000 with a high school diploma. Someone with a bachelor's degree makes on average $47,000. The degree costs about $80,000. This equates to a bachelor's degree costing you about double a years' worth of salary.

Some companies are seeing that they need to pay people better wages. Target is making the move to $15 an hour by 2020. They understand that they need to raise their wages to attract and retain top talent. Target is showing everyone that it can be done. When you pay people a decent wage, you are helping the company as well as the economy. Higher wages will lead to higher employee retention as well as higher productivity. This will also lead to increased spending into the economy.

78% of Americans are living paycheck to paycheck. 43% of Americans struggle making less than $15 an hour. Overall, most workers are in debt and believe they always will be. Most financial experts recommend having a six-month cushion as an emergency fund. How can Americans save when they don't make a livable wage? Wages have not been keeping up with cost of living in decades. In Stockton, California, their Mayor, Michael Tubbs, has an idea that seems crazy to some. Starting in 2019, his city is going to provide a monthly stipend/guaranteed income ($500) to a group of residents as part of an 18-month experiment. Tubbs stated he "felt almost a moral responsibility to do something a little bit out of the box" for his city of 300,000. Only will time will tell how this guaranteed income will help Stockton.[27]

Capitalism by itself is not inherently bad. In fact, it is what has allowed amazing advances in our technology. But we have allowed myths like greed is good by allowing tax cuts for companies to make the market work. Today, corporations believe they must be run to maximize shareholder value. By running the companies this way, they are keeping the rich…rich and the poor….poor.

> **Capitalism:** An economic and political system in which a country's trade and industry are controlled by private owners for profit, rather than by the state

In the 1980s, large companies spent less than 50% of their earnings on shareholders while spending more on their employees. Looking into the 2010s, we now see companies dedicated more than 80% to 90% of their earnings to shareholders. Companies are now only concerned about their shareholder value maximization. To help combat these issues, Senator Elizabeth Warren has created the Accountable Capitalism Act, which would restore American corporations to work for all major stakeholders, which includes their own employees. This approach follows the "Benefit Corporation" model, which is being used by such successful companies as Patagonia and Kickstarter.

Now you may say that that is a liberal idea and it will never work. Well, even conservative Florida senator Marco Rubio penned his own op-ed on how America needs to restore dignity

---

[27]Ross, "California."

of work. This is not a partisan issue. Marco states, "If hardworking Americans don't have stable jobs that pay enough to buy a home and raise a family, our nation is in very serious trouble."[28] He also mentions ending the tax code's favoritism for companies that spend their tax cuts on stock buybacks and that labor unions decline has been bad for the U.S.

51% of young adults (18 to 29) no longer support the system of capitalism. This trend can be seen in other countries as well, such as England and Germany. So why do young adults dislike capitalism so much? It is simple: they have grown up seeing how these monopolies are using and abusing their parents to grow their stock price and give their executives higher wages. They also see that these companies don't voluntarily do the right thing, like increasing wages above poverty levels or stopping their own pollution. They see people working too many hours and not making a decent wage no matter how hard they try. They likely have gone through one or both of their parents or other family members getting laid off, even when they were a top performer the year before. They believe big companies do not care about their employees; they care about profit.

Today, companies are viewing labor just like a roll of toilet paper or a pencil. Where can they can get the cheapest person? Companies are not always looking for the most qualified, they want the cheapest they can find. Employees are taking these lower wages because they have bills to pay. Employers see employees as expendable to companies instead of trying to retain talent by paying a good living. Companies have forgotten how to

---

[28]Rubio, "America."

compensate workers fairly, so they constantly have the same job openings available. Any given day, Walmart has job openings at most of their stores. Companies would rather spend their money on training new employees, than take that money to keep the good employees they have. How has this become normalized as being ok?

Workers need to step up and demand more money because the U.S. has had over 100 straight months of jobs growth (as of April 2019). Companies need to realize why it is taking longer and longer to fill their open jobs; their lower pay and benefits. Yes, there are some skill gaps, but skills can be taught and people would be willing to learn on the job if the pay was decent. Companies need to step up and become part of the solution instead of complaining they cannot find employees. They have caused this gap because of their greed. Now is the time to realize greed isn't what is needed. Compassion and companies who want their employees to succeed is.

Like I have said before, we are an apathetic instant gratification nation. We shop at stores like Walmart because we think they are giving us the lowest priced products when they don't anymore. I can find cheaper items in many local stores compared to Walmart. So, Walmart isn't the cheapest and they don't pay their workers a livable wage while their CEO keeps making huge bonuses. We are spending our hard-earned money at a company that continues the income inequality in the U.S. Walmart is Fortune's #1 company because they made $14.69 billion profit in 2016. Yet they start their employees at $9 to $12 an hour, which is not a livable wage. We need to stop thinking these jobs are just steppingstones for employees.

Companies such as Walmart and Amazon don't always offer full-time work with benefits to their employees. Average hours per week can be around 30.

- A single Walmart Supercenter can cost taxpayers between $904,542 and $1.75 million per year in public assistance money.
- In some states, Walmart and Amazon employees are the largest group of Medicaid recipients.
- Walmart and Amazon employees are also the single biggest group of Supplemental Nutrition Assistance Program (SNAP) recipients. In other words, those everyday low prices at the chain are, in part, subsidized by your tax money.
- Walmart and Amazon accept SNAP, thus making more money off of the government.

Income inequality doesn't just affect people's paychecks. It also affects their life expectancy. Poor Americans are dying earlier while the rich are enjoying longevity. Average life expectancy has declined for two years in a row for the average American. Most of this is due to the staggering healthcare costs and access to medical care. Most wealthy countries (such as France, Australia, and Canada) believe that healthcare is a right, while the U.S. treats healthcare as a privilege for people who can pay for it. All while companies keep employees from working full time, so they can't qualify for health insurance. The Affordable Care Act (ACA) was developed to help with this issue, but until the U.S. steps up to a universal healthcare system, this trend will continue. Capitalism has proven that companies would rather not give health insurance or if they do, they can make it expensive for the employee, so the companies can make more profits.

Think about how many dollar stores you have seen pop up in lower income areas as rural America continues to struggle. There are more than 30,000 dollar stores in the U.S., which is up from 18,000 a decade ago. Dollar General and Dollar Tree are expanding by approximately 1,000 more locations per year. Did you know that both of these stores carry groceries? Have you bought a dollar store steak yet? Even the CEO of Dollar General told the *Wall Street Journal* that "the economy is continuing to create more of our core customer,"[29] which if you haven't figured out is the struggling American.

Do you think any of these stores that keep growing into the rural areas are paying livable wages? You would be right if you said no. These companies are coming into these communities and bringing lower-paying jobs for people who will, in turn, spend their money back at the same store. In some small towns, the dollar store is their only place for groceries, including fresh fruits and vegetables. When you live somewhere where you can choose between dozens of options, you don't realize that many areas of our country don't have any options for their grocery needs. They have one place they can go.

In the book *Enough*, John Bogle dives into the true measures of money, business, and life. In the past 30 to 40 years, we have changed significantly from the country that cared about the masses into only caring about a few. Ethical professionalism has been lacking and we must strive to return to professional values. Capitalism must be fair, regulated, and ethical. While wealth,

---

[29]Pandey, "Dollar stores."

fame, and power are all attributes to success, they are flawed measures of success. "Success cannot be measured solely—or even primarily—in monetary terms, nor in terms of the amount of power one may exercise over others, nor in the illusory fame of inevitably transitory public notice. But it can be measured in our contributions to building a better world, in helping our fellow man, and in raising children who themselves become loving human beings and good citizens. Success, in short, can be measured not in what we attain for ourselves, but in what we contribute to our society."[30]

It is time to change the narrative of what we as a society deem as success. Today we admire people who have the most money and the most things. But we used to admire people who developed new life-saving drugs and were humanitarians who helped people. Who should be our role models?

In the book *The Common Good*, Robert Reich dives into three parts: What is the common good? What happened to the common good? Can the common good be restored?[31] We have become a country where greed rules. Examples include pharmaceuticals changing pill prices from $13.50 to $750, too-big-to-fail banks failing and needing a government bailout (that they never paid back to the taxpayers), and don't forget about investors using Ponzi schemes to steal your money. This has become normal and to hell with the common good.

The constitution was designed for We the People not for the top 1%. But by 2016, corporations and Wall Street contributed $34 for every $1 donated by labor unions and all public interest

---

[30]Bogle, *Enough.*
[31]Reich, *The Common Good.*

organizations combined to lobbying. This is due to a verdict by the Supreme Court (Citizens United case) that corporations are people.[32,33,34] We must get this money out of politics because businesses are not citizens. To lead us back to the common good, we need leadership as trusteeship, honor and shame, resurrecting truth, and civic education for all.

> "We cannot be effective citizens in the democracy if truths unfavorable to those with power are suppressed, while lies favorable to them are offered as truth."
>
> **—Robert Reich**
> Former Secretary of Labor

Before we leave this subject, I believe it is very important to point out correlations that I have found in my state of Florida.

- Walmart is largest private employer ($9 to $12 an hour to start)
- The Equal Rights Amendment was never passed
- Right to Work state (unions are bad for business)
- Highest in income inequality
- 46th in education
- Substandard public transportation
- Most politically biased

---

[32]Drutman, "Lobbyists."
[33]Wikipedia, "Citizens United v. FEC."
[34]Dunbar, "Citizens United."

Florida wants to keep their population

1. Uneducated
2. Poor (non-union) to keep wages lower
3. Politically biased to keep them uneducated and poor

I hope that Florida can stop hurting themselves and open their eyes to the truth. After Hurricane Michael devastated the town of Panama City, some businesses that reopened dropped wages because they knew people needed work because they lost everything in the storm. As the cost of living skyrocketed in this community due to little to no available housing, most wages have not increased. This is our reality. I'm personally working in my community to increase wages because no one should have to work 80 hours a week to afford to live in a one-bedroom apartment.

Imagine if the state of Florida raised its minimum wage to $15, added better public transportation, and focused on making the public education system better (not just charter schools). Their citizens would have more money, education, and a higher standard of living. Then maybe they would be able to have more time to get involved locally and help their communities. All change starts at the local level and the state of Florida doesn't like that. In the 2019 session of the Florida government they are trying to take away local city rights because they don't want cities to raise the minimum wage, protect the LGBTQ+ community, or even protect their own environment. Instead, Florida wants to give more money to for-profit charter schools instead of public education, arm teachers, and—my favorite—make all Florida residents Immigration and Customs Enforcement (ICE) agents by making it a crime to not report anyone who is suspected of being undocumented. This is our reality in 2019.

KRT Recap:

Our history is messy and complicated. For us to build a business or society that works for all, we must recognize what got us here and change for the future. If we were leading with kindness, wouldn't all employees have a livable wage? If we were leading with kindness, would we still discriminate and pay unequally? The answer is a resounding **NO**. Our greed, hate, and fear have led us down a path that is no longer feasible. We cannot continue operating the way we have been. This is why the KRT model is so important for our future.

By leading with kindness, we will not only be changing our workforce, we will also be changing our society. We will develop more empathy and compassion for our fellow humans. In turn, this compassion will lead more respect for each other and our differences. Ultimately, we will achieve unprecedented levels of trust in organizations. Imagine what your organization can accomplish when its employees feel the psychological safety to be fearless?

2

THE BAD AND UGLY

Before we begin this chapter, I want you to think about these questions: Have you ever had a bad boss? Have you ever been told by Human Resources that you were over-reacting? Have you ever seen women silenced in a meeting? Have you ever seen discrimination or been discriminated against at your job? I know my answer to these questions are yes, yes, yes, and yes. These types of actions and behaviors are not conducive to a productive workplace, yet we allow them to keep occurring. This is exactly why the Kindness, Respect, and Trust model is needed.

ADULT BULLIES

Employees really don't like working for Adult Bullies. They don't want to work in hostile work environments. They don't want to feel like they are in high school with all the cliques. They don't want bosses who refuse to teach and help. **They want someone to connect with them and treat them with kindness and respect.**

Bullying can affect everyone including witnesses. Bullying is linked to health impacts such as mental health issues, substance abuse, and even suicide. We focus on bullying being about children, but we don't look at it as much with adults. It is a problem and we need to learn more.

There are different types of Adult Bullies (per Bullyingstatistics. org):[35]

- **Narcissistic Adult Bully:** Self-centered, no empathy, little anxiety about consequences. He or she seems to feel good about him or herself but has a brittle narcissism that requires putting others down.
- **Impulsive Adult Bully:** More spontaneous and does not plan their bullying. He or she has a hard time restraining his or her behavior and, in some cases, it can be unintentional.
- **Physical Bully:** Adults rarely turn to physical confrontation. They use the threat of harm or physical domination. They may damage or steal a victim's property rather than physically confronting them.
- **Verbal Adult Bully:** Starts rumors or uses sarcastic or demeaning language to dominate or humiliate another person. This subtle type of bullying also has the advantage—to the bully—of being difficult to document. The emotional and psychological impacts of verbal bullying can be felt quite keenly and can result in reduced job performance and even depression.
- **Secondary Adult Bully:** This is someone who does not initiate the bullying but joins in so that he or she does not become a victim. They feel bad but want to protect themselves.

---

[35]Bullying Statistics.

Adult Bullies are most interested in domination and power. They could have grown up with strict father morality but 100% grew up within the patriarchal society we live in. They do not care about the effects of their actions and enjoy calling people names. They cause hostile toxic work environments that disrupt work production, morale, and overall Net Promoter Score (NPS).

KRT In Action—A Tale of Two Managers example

J and B are managers in a call center. J likes being #1 and will do anything to keep that spot. B wants to be #1 and believes the team is the key. In their daily meetings, J calls out the bad sellers in front of the whole team to shame them. B congratulates the team for their previous day and sets goals for that day.

During the day, J walks around and yells when someone hasn't had a sale yet while B sits with their team members and works through their roadblocks to increased sales. At the end of the day, J sits in their office while their team leaves while B is saying goodnight to their team and is making things personal.

KRT Recap

B is showing the characteristics of a leader while J is just being an Adult Bully. It's easy to see the difference when a team is being led with kindness.

Who do you believe is the better manager? Which team do you want to be on?

J is a manager in the workplace who is only out for him/herself. B, on the other hand, has figured out that to help her/himself be number one, her/his team will be the one to get her/him there. J's old-school tactics may have worked in the past, but with Gen Y (millennials) and Gen Z in the workforce, these tactics are no longer going to work. The newer generations won't settle for this disrespect. Why do you think millennials aren't staying in jobs? It's probably because their boss was like J. *No one wants a manager who is an Adult Bully and screams at them.*

This example occurs every day. We have been taught that having a boss like J is normal. It is not ok to yell and scream at people. It is not ok to treat people differently for any reason. Having a manager who does not care about their team is not good for any business.

Adult Bully managers promote people not qualified for the job because of favoritism. They want to keep people around them who will help keep their power. In other words, they need followers and people who will praise them for this behavior. Human Resources allows this Adult Bully behavior, which leads to toxic hostile work environments.

> **Hostile Work Environments** exist when one's behavior within a workplace creates an environment that is difficult for another person to work in.

As Human Resources keeps allowing these bad behaviors, we might wonder why companies keep allowing their toxic people to thrive. According to a 2015 study published by the Harvard Business School, the data shows that these toxic employees drive other employees to leave an organization faster and more frequently. Their behavior is contagious and can cause other team members to behave in a toxic fashion. While these toxic employees may be more productive than the average worker, they will harm the bottom line in the end.[36] It is not worth any company to allow these bad behaviors.

It is time we expose this behavior for what it is. Report all of it to Human Resources. Every time—even if it is every day. And, if you are in a position of leadership, you need to call out the individual when they are acting like an Adult Bully and tell them that their behavior is not appropriate and will not be tolerated in the workplace. Most companies have a code of business conduct that states this type of behavior is against their policies. We need to force Human Resources to do their job and stop these Adult Bullies.

"If you are neutral in situations of injustice, you have chosen the side of the oppressor. If an elephant has its foot on a tail of a mouse and you say that you are neutral, the mouse will not appreciate your neutrality."

—Bishop Desmond Tutu
Nobel Peace Prize winner

When there are weeks and months and years of data against someone for being an Adult Bully and causing a hostile work

---

[36]Bookbinder, "Toxic Workers."

environment, don't you wonder why that employee still has their job? There are no career obstacles for these incompetent bullies. We are living in a system that rewards bad behaviors while damaging great employees.

Have you heard of the Workplace Bullying Institute (WBI)? Here are their key findings for 2017.[37]

Key Findings

- 19% of Americans are bullied, another 19% witness it
- 61% of Americans are aware of abusive conduct in the workplace
- 60.4 million Americans are affected by it
- 70% of perpetrators are men; 60% of targets are women
- Hispanics are the most frequently bullied race
- 61% of bullies are bosses, the majority (63%) operate alone
- 40% of bullied targets are believed to suffer adverse health effects
- 29% of targets remain silent about their experiences
- 71% of employer reactions are harmful to targets
- 60% of coworker reactions are harmful to targets
- To stop it, 65% of targets lose their original jobs
- 77% of Americans support enacting a new law
- 46% report worsening of work relationships, post-2016 election

---

Do any of these findings surprise you?

Did you know there is a Healthy Workplace Campaign to create a bill to help combat these Adult Bullies?[38]

---

[37]Workplace Bullying Institute.
[38]Healthy Workplace Campaign.

Quick Facts About the Healthy Workplace Bill (HWB)

What the HWB Does for Employers

- Precisely defines an "abusive work environment"—it is a high standard for misconduct
- Requires proof of health harm by licensed health or mental health professionals
- Protects conscientious employers from vicarious liability risk when internal correction and prevention mechanisms are in effect
- Gives employers the reason to terminate or sanction offenders
- Requires plaintiffs to use private attorneys
- Plugs the gaps in current state and federal civil rights protections

What the HWB Does for Workers

- Provides an avenue for legal redress for health harming cruelty at work
- Allows you to sue the bully as an individual
- Holds the employer accountable
- Seeks restoration of lost wages and benefits
- Compels employers to prevent and correct future instances

What the HWB Does Not Do

- Involves state agencies to enforce any provisions of the law
- Incurs costs for adopting states
- Requires plaintiffs to be members of protected status groups (it is "status-blind")
- Uses the term "workplace bullying"

While this bill is a start in the right direction, it really isn't going to fix the underlying problem. We need to stop pretending that Adult Bullies don't exist. Even if you have not had to deal with any of these issues, it does not mean they do not exist. Do a little experiment: Ask a stranger on the street if their boss yells at them or they have seen discrimination in their job. The numbers seem to average over 50%. Some days I have even gotten up 90%. That means more than 50% of Americans see the problem. They believe the problem is normal and that is how businesses work. ***IT IS NOT NORMAL.*** This is not how companies should operate.

There are a lot of different tactics that Adult Bullies use to keep their power. Obnoxious aggression is one of those tactics. This is when someone goes straight into criticizing someone. People may feel like this is the way to provide feedback, but you just come off as a jerk. This type of feedback is belittling and emotionally draining for the person taking the feedback. In fact, some bosses target people so they can assert their dominance and show them who is the boss. Obnoxious aggression is a behavior not a personality trait. This type of behavior should not be allowed in business and Human Resources needs to be conscious that this type of behavior exists and needs to know how to combat and stop it.

People who work for managers who yell at them are:

- More likely to have anxiety/depression
- Less productive at work
- More likely to take sick days when not sick
- Less likely to stay in their job

Share your Adult Bully stories at www.stopgreednow.com

KRT INACTION—A TALE OF AN ADULT BULLY

Shelly was a team player and on salary (no overtime). Her coworker Dale just left for a new job. Her manager thought it would be a good idea to give Shelly all of Dale's work. Shelly, being a team player, took on Dale's reporting job and continued with all her other duties. The reports were very tedious and had to be created with precision and care each morning. Shelly got to work at 5 a.m. each day to make sure the report was out by 8 a.m. Shelly worked each night until 7 p.m. or 8 p.m. to make sure everything else got done.

One day, when running the reports, the net increase in sales was negative. Shelly had never seen this before but knew (based on previous days) that the disconnect department did not process any orders for at least one to two days. Shelly concluded that the backlog of disconnects must have been processed the previous day, which led to the negative numbers. Shelly called her director, Faira, and let her know what was going on. Faira told Shelly not to publish the report and send out an email stating the report had problems and would not be published that day.

Within ten minutes, Shelly got a call from her vice president, Terrance. Terrance started yelling and wanting to know why the report wasn't going out. Shelly followed the story that her director told her to state "that there were problems and the report would not be published today". Terrance continued to probe with accusatory statements and tried to blame Shelly. At this point, Shelly told him to call Faira and talk with her. He hung up without saying a word.

Shelly started to get scared that she did the wrong thing, even though it was what her director told her to do. Faira called five minutes later and stated that she told Terrance that the numbers were off, and they needed to investigate it, even though she knew the truth.

Shelly took all the blame because her Adult Bully director and vice president didn't want to state the truth on how the end of month numbers were manipulated. They wanted the largest net gain for the end of the quarter to make investors happy. Even the legal department signed off on manipulating the numbers.

KRT Recap

You can easily see how the company was setting up Shelly for failure. Faira was not being truthful to her boss even though she knew the truth. If the KRT model was being used, Shelly would have never been put in this lie. The truth would have been told and the VP would not have blamed Shelly.

Do you think Shelly did the right thing?

Shelly was in a very difficult position caused by her manager. She knew what happened and reported it, but it didn't matter. The report would make the company look bad, so her director thought it would be easier to lie than face the truth that the company caused their own issues. They didn't process the accounts to be disconnected because they wanted to make sure their end of month/quarter sales numbers were higher. What do you do when you are afraid you are going to lose your job if you don't do exactly as your boss stated?

These types of scenarios happen all too often in the business world. Everyone is trying to cover their own ass, instead of stepping up to the truth. Adult Bullies can make you do things because they threaten your job and gaslight you. They want to be in control and if, at any time, you don't follow directions, you could be without a job. Why isn't Human Resources doing anything to help?

We have come to the point that this behavior has been normalized and people are thinking it is ok. ***THIS IS NOT OK.*** We have normalized this behavior by creating hundreds of ways (articles) to deal with your boss yelling. There is even a wikiHow on how to survive a hostile work environment.

Is meanness and bullying winning in business? Leaders of the Fortune 500 companies will say no. But they are just pretending to not know about the issues. According to a Pew Research report, 41% of people online have experienced bullying online, harassment, and intimidation.[39] These tactics disproportionally affect women, people of color, and LGBTQ+. So, when leaders say they don't know, then they are just plain liars. They know, and they still let it happen. They choose making money over acting like human beings.

Dr. Gary Namie stated it best in his quote in the article "Workplace-Bullying Laws on the Horizon" from Society for Human Resource Management (SHRM):[40] "Abuse in the workplace is the last form of abuse not considered taboo in the U.S.," he said. "In practice, workplace bullying is domestic violence at work, where the abuser is on the payroll. The longer we delay, the more workers who don't deserve denigrating abuse suffer."

GASLIGHTING

Gaslighting has been used for years, but recently there has been more reporting on this tactic. This tactic is very scary because

---

[39]Duggan, "Harassment."

[40]Maurer, "Workplace-Bullying Laws."

anyone is susceptible. People don't even realize that it is happening to them. Human Resources does not know how to handle the situation.

> **Gaslighting:** A form of mental abuse in which information is twisted or spun, selectively omitted to favor the abuser, or false information is presented with the intent of making victims doubt their own memory, perception, and sanity.

I have been gaslighted. I bet you have been, too. The hardest part is that you are made to feel like you imagined what happened. The gaslighters will keep telling their version of the story so many times, you will question whether you remember things correctly. The point is to keep you confused and delegitimize your beliefs and feelings.

> *"If you tell a lie long enough and loud enough it becomes the truth."*
>
> **—Adolph Hitler**
> Leader of the Nazi party

According to "Gaslighting: Know it and identify it to protect yourself" published in *Psychology Today*, here are a few techniques people use:[41]

---

[41] Sarkis, "Gaslighting."

- They tell you blatant lies and will deny they ever said something, even though you have proof
- They use what is near and dear to you as ammunition and wear you down over time
- Their actions do not match their words and they know confusion weakens people
- They throw in positive reinforcement to confuse you
- They try to align people against you and tell you or others that you are crazy
- They tell you everyone else is a liar

KRT Inaction—Gaslighting example

Chi has worked for the same business for 12 years. She has worked her way up to a director position. She joins a new part of the business to launch a new product. During the year, she is subjected to a host of different issues such as discrimination/sexism, misogyny, bias, bigotry, prejudice, and sexual harassment. She works for an Adult Bully who has created a hostile work environment. She takes her concerns to her manager's boss—an executive vice president (EVP)—who, in turn, decides that it would be easier to gaslight Chi instead of dealing with the issues.

Chi did not realize she was being gaslighted. Her manager was moved to a new job and now Chi reports directly to the EVP. Chi was nominated for the top manager award and won. The EVP did this to confuse Chi and have Chi stop caring about the other problems. This also aligned other employees against Chi because they wanted the award.

The problems did not go away, and Chi spoke to her EVP about the issues weekly. But this time, Chi understood that her EVP was a female misogynist and made sure to document everything. The EVP told Chi she was crazy and the issues weren't that bad. She needed to deal with it or quit her job. Chi knew that the company had a business code of conduct, which specifically stated these behaviors were not allowed.

Chi took her documented issues to Human Resources. Human Resources did nothing to help the situation, they didn't even bother to respond for almost six months. The gaslighting continued until Chi could no longer work in that environment. Chi went to a different job. The EVP and all the people involved in the issues still have their jobs and are allowed to continue this behavior.

KRT Recap

Chi's managers were allowed to continue bad behaviors while Human Resources condoned and basically approved of them. If the KRT model was being used, the company would not have allowed any of this behavior to be normalized. Human Resources would have actually done the right thing.

When Human Resources does nothing to help, a person being gaslighted feels like they have nowhere to turn. Most of my business career, I have had women give me advice on how to be a better leader. Some of this advice was just to gaslight me to be compliant in a patriarchal workplace. I was told to be certain ways and to act certain ways. All in the name of providing feedback to help me advance my career. We will get into this more in the Women Leaders section.

Gaslighting is abuse. Check out YouTube for many different videos to help you recognize and help stop gaslighting in your professional and personal life.

Gaslighting exploits people's need for connection and belonging. It undermines the person's emotions and, in effect, denies their reality. Gaslighting makes a person think they are too sensitive, crazy, and unhappy. It makes a person wonder if they are good enough and they will even make excuses for the gaslighters' behavior.

Phrases you may hear from gaslighters are:

- You are too sensitive.
- Don't get so upset.
- You are overreacting.
- You are insecure.
- I was just joking!
- You are imagining things.
- It's no big deal.

Do you usually hear these types of phrases from one person? Are you having a stressful conversation about your job, money, infidelity, sex, or family? Recognizing you are having a gaslighting problem and sorting out the truth from distortion is a great first step. Once you recognize what is happening then you can make the necessary changes to stop the behavior.

Gaslighting
is not
normal.

While gaslighting can occur from anyone, we need to focus on how it has been allowed to continue as normal in companies. We need to step back and wonder what happened to the golden rule (treat people how you want to be treated or how you would treat your mother). Why do businesses allow this behavior? Where is Human Resources when you need them? Why have a business code of conduct when companies don't follow it?

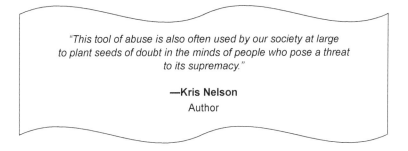

"This tool of abuse is also often used by our society at large to plant seeds of doubt in the minds of people who pose a threat to its supremacy."

—Kris Nelson
Author

Here's is my revolutionary idea, are you ready?

Human Resources should grow a backbone and stop allowing this behavior. They believe the victims. They watch for patterns of abuse. Workplaces shouldn't be this way and we can change this.

HUMAN RESOURCES IS A PROBLEM

In the 1980s when companies changed their Personnel Departments into Human Resources departments, everything changed. That is when

Human Resources started treating employees as numbers instead of as human beings. This shift has led to bad policies and many lawsuits that could have been avoided. Employees are the backbone of any business and when businesses lose sight of that, they are failing.

> *"We should take a minute out of our day to look into the faces of the people we manage. And to realize that they are most important resources."*
>
> **—Kenneth Blanchard and Spence Johnson**
> Influential Leadership Experts/Authors

Human Resources has a lot of power, but they lost their way in all the greed-based decisions, thanks to the executives. They are not making decisions to help employees. They are making decisions about people by looking at a spreadsheet and deciding by department how many people they need to lose. I understand businesses must go through transitions and let people go. But it is being done all wrong. Good people and great employees are losing their jobs because Human Resources is taking the easy way out.

Human Resources allows Adult Bullies to get their way. If an employee is viewed as not adapting to the bad culture, they are identified as a problem and the Human Resources person teams with the Adult Bully to work* the employee out of the business (*Fancy way of saying finding a way to fire the employee legally by making sure they fail.) If they do receive complaints about the Adult Bully, they gaslight the employee into thinking it is all their fault or they don't respond at all. Human Resources sees the hostile work environment and does nothing to stop it because they are of the mentality: if you don't like it leave.

How do big businesses do their layoffs?

KRT Inaction—Layoff/Surplus situation example

Human Resources comes in and provides guidance. This guidance is what leads to who gets fired and who gets to stay.

- Bob is gone due to being the newest member of the team, even though he is the highest ranked member
- Alexandra is gone because she is rated low because her manager doesn't like her because she is a woman
- Rob is gone because he has the highest salary on the team and is over 60
- Tamara is gone because she is not a team player and transgender
- Kelli is gone due to being rated low because she was out on disability last year due to a surgery that was approved by the business

---

In this example, the Human Resources department gave the departments different information to make their decisions and they allowed Adult Bully behavior to decide who gets laid off. Does Human Resources even realize they are doing this? They are making it so employees cannot find an internal transfer because they are on the layoff/surplus list, which means they are no good at their job based on people's opinions (stereotype/bias). All because the company does not care to do things the right way. Imagine if an employee was treated with the same respect as the C-Suite executives?

All of this stupidity reminds me of a few Dilbert cartoons from the *Dilbert Principle* book.[42] The *Dilbert Principle* may have

---

[42]Adams, *The Dilbert Principle.*

been written in 1996, but there is still so much truth to the absurdity it shows about business.

Cartoon 1: Pointy-Haired Boss talking to Dilbert and a lady

Pointy-Haired Boss: Our CEO is announcing a 10% staff reduction to cut expenses.

Dilbert: Question: Didn't our CEO get paid $20 million this year?

Pointy-Haired Boss: Yes, but risky jobs deserve higher pay.

Dilbert: Question: Didn't you say we were getting cut?

Pointy-Haired Boss: The staff cuts will be determined by tossing a dart at the organization chart while blindfolded. Throws dart.

Lady: You slayed Johnson.

Pointy-Haired Boss: Boy, talk about decisive management.

Cartoon 2: Catbert talking to Pointy-Haired Boss

Catbert: I hired a new director of human resources to handle the downsizing.

Catbert: I needed somebody who acts like a friend but secretly delights in the misery of all people.

Catbert: We need to talk, Paul. But first I'm going to bat your head around and scratch you.

Paul: Hee Hee! That's so cute.

It has been over 23 years since those cartoons were published, yet nothing really has changed. If there is to be real change, then Human Resources needs to step up and look at how they have caused the problems. They need to deploy the KRT model to shift their focus more to the employees and what is truly going on within the company. These changes will take time. Human Resources needs to put their gloves on and tackle the bad culture that is running their business. Human Resources needs to hold managers accountable for their actions. Shouldn't the Board of Directors and shareholders demand better for employees?

Examples of behavior that Human Resources condones and allows:

- When hiring, Human Resources/management asks what race/gender is the person who is being hired
- Allowing gender/race pay gap to continue:
  - Offering men more than women
  - Offering white men more than people of color
  - Offering straight white men more than an LGBTQ+
- Allowing harassment (real statements)
  - "Her boobs are bigger than her brain"
  - "You look hot today in those heels"
  - "I need to tap that ass"
  - "Your opinion doesn't matter because you are black, women, gay, transgender, stupid, etc."
  - "You are gay, so you can't understand"
- Add your own example—there are many to choose from

Imagine if all hiring was done without knowing the gender of the person. Orchestras around the world are doing that now. They understand that they have a bias problem. In the late 1970s, just 5% of orchestra members were women. Now it is well into 30%. The only difference they made was the blind audition. They even had to go as far as have women not wear heels because that clickity clack of the heels gave away their gender and biased the judges. With a blind audition, you are assessing a person's talents based on the talent and not what they looked like.

I know we want to think this type of behavior does not occur. We want to believe that we as society are better than this. *The fact is that we are not.* This behavior has been allowed to occur. But it doesn't have to be this way. I know that we need to stop these bad behaviors. We can make this positive change together. Are you with me?

KRT Inaction—Adult Bully/Misogyny Example

Margo has been a manager for the same business for 20 years. She leads by fear and intimidation. No one wants to work in Margo's team because they are afraid they will get fired if they disagree with Margo. Margo always raises her voice in meetings and enjoys that people fear her.

Margo had over 100 complaints submitted to Human Resources over three years. Margo was required to attend sensitivity training and had her raises/bonuses taken away for two years. Margo attended the training and made all the changes needed to become a better manager.

Nathan has been a manager at the same business as Margo for 15 years. He leads by fear and intimidation. Only men want to work on Nathan's team because they like his hard stance. Nathan raises his voice in most meetings because he knows he will command respect by doing so.

Nathan has had just as many complaints as Margo but has not been required to take any training or lose any pay.

KRT Recap

It's easy to see that no one in this example was using the KRT model. If the KRT model was being used, this type of double standard would not have occurred. In fact, both managers would have been sent to training much earlier than over three years of complaints.

The example above shows two different leaders who act the same way but are treated totally differently. Why does Human Resources allow men to get away with bad behavior, but make women take training? Why did it take three years and over 100 complaints for Human Resources to act?

Hold Human Resources accountable

Seriously, aren't you tired of the double standards? Aren't you tired of the sexism, racism, homophobia and all the discriminations that still occur? I know I am. I'm tired of the oppressed being blamed for calling out the nature of the oppression. It's time to create the culture that is inclusive. Where everyone cares and has the courage to speak up against the bad behaviors and Adult Bullies. Where we have the psychological safety to know that when we speak up we will be listened to.

What gets measured is what a company focuses on. We need to start measuring how we treat our employees, how we are running our companies, and what truly is the main thing. We have lost ourselves. We have allowed our own confirmation bias and cognitive dissonance to keep us from doing the right thing.

> *"The time is always right to do what is right."*
>
> **—Martin Luther King Jr.**
> Civil Rights Activist and Minister

So, let's make some changes. Let's create the New KRT Rules for Human Resources.

New KRT Rules for Human Resources

- End all discrimination and unequal pay
    - Audit all employees' pay based on their titles and make appropriate changes. Make the reports public.
    - Companies need to sign an equal pay pledge.
- End hostile work environments by disallowing/firing the Adult Bullies, misogynists, racists, et al.
    - Audit all Human Resources complaints on managers and take appropriate actions. Make the reports public.
- Stand up for/protect employees
    - Stop gaslighting and allowing managers to degrade employees.
    - Stop victim-blaming.
    - Create psychological safety.
- Drive a productive culture through diversity and inclusion.
    - Look at all parts of the business (including upper management) and make sure there is diversity.
    - Diversity includes everyone - all races, genders, sexual orientation and age.
- Create sexual harassment training that works.
- Create a Code of Honor (Ethics) for employees.
    - Create a culture of inclusion.
    - Disallow cheating – make reports public.
    - Reward people for telling the truth and taking risks.

Creating a Code of Honor will lead to a more ethical, honest company. Within this code of honor, all employees and management will no longer allow dishonesty. Managers will be looked at based on how many Human Resource complaints have come in on them and why. Lastly, making it transparent to everyone changes the accountability structure.

Code of Honor: Set of rules or ethical principles governing a business community based on ideals that define what constitutes acceptable behavior within that business/community.

Imagine a world with employees who are happy to be at work. Imagine a company that is willing to step up and make the changes needed. Imagine a society that won't allow Adult Bullies or any bad behaviors. Imagine a CEO who is willing to take the risk. Imagine what our world would become.

Detailed information and exercises about the New Rules for Human Resources can be found at www.bekindtoall.com

DISCRIMINATION/BIAS/STEREOTYPES

Discrimination: The unjust or prejudicial treatment of different categories of people or things; especially on the grounds of race, age, and sex (sexual orientation).

Facts:

- All discriminations still exist
- Equal pay for equal work is joke
- Being an Adult Bully by yelling and screaming is commonplace
- Managers who get reported for bad behaviors don't have any consequences

You may be thinking: hey there are laws for many of these items. The U.S. Equal Employment Opportunity Commission (EEOC) was created to enforce federal laws that make it illegal to discriminate against a job applicant or an employee because of the following:

- Race
- Color
- Religion
- Sex (including pregnancy, gender identity, sexual orientation interpreted by EEOC to be included but not federal law)
- National origin
- Age (40 or older)
- Disability
- Genetic information

It is also illegal to discriminate against a person because the person complained about discrimination, filed a charge of discrimination, or participated in an employment discrimination investigation or lawsuit.

The EEOC has the authority to investigate charges of discrimination against employers who are covered by the law. They investigate to fairly and accurately assess the allegations in the charge and then make a finding. The EEOC has the authority to file a lawsuit to protect the rights of individuals and the interests of the public. They do not file lawsuits in all cases where they find discrimination. Total number of charges filed by year:

- 2017: 84,254
- 2016: 91,503
- 2015: 89,385
- 2014: 88,778
- 2013: 93,727
- 2012: 99,412
- 2011: 99,947

As the data shows, the number of EEOC charges are lower than 2011. **Is this because more businesses are following the laws, or is it because people aren't filing charges?**

Employees are taking matters in their own hands and are leaving the jobs where discrimination occurs. Most are not filing any charges because they have left the company and don't want to be involved anymore. Since it's up to the victim (employee) to prove that that the business is discriminating, why would anyone report the behavior if they no longer work there?

Per the American Psychological Association (APA), nearly seven out of ten adults have experienced discrimination in their lives.[43] There are over 329 million people in the U.S., so why was the number of charges less than .02% of the population in 2015? The truth is that people are not reporting the discrimination issues and the statistics are not correct. The issue is much larger than the data suggests.

---

[43]Lane, "Discrimination."

This is where we are today. The question is where do we want to be? To get to this answer, we must be very truthful about our current society. We have to dig into what we have been taught. We have to look at ourselves and decide who we really are as people. Saying you don't discriminate but letting discrimination occur in front of you means you discriminate. Neutrality is support for the status quo.

Take five minutes and answer these questions honestly:

- Do you judge people for handling a situation differently than you would?
- Do you have friends who are not the same color, religion, sexual orientation that you are?
- Do you jump to a stereotype or bias when you see someone?
- Do you label people or talk about them behind their backs?
- Do you hire certain people over others?
- How diverse is your team?
  - How many men versus women?
  - How many people who aren't white?
  - How many people are not like you? (socially/politically/culturally)
  - How many people who were not men have you promoted?
- Do you believe that all humans deserve kindness?
- Do you use microaggressions?

Has our society been engrained with stereotypes and bias? **YES.**

Implicit Bias: An attitude that always favors one way of feeling or acting especially without considering any other possibilities.

> **Unconscious Bias** is when discrimination and incorrect judg-
> ments occur due to stereotyping. These can occur automatically
> and without the person being aware of it.

How you grew up and your experiences have paved the way to who you are today. If you have always had money, then you have no idea about a person who has been living paycheck to paycheck their entire life. It's hard to face the fact that all of us have these behaviors, whether we want to or not. *Implicit and unconscious bias affects everyone—whether we realize it or not.*

Do you find yourself treating the person serving you at McDonald's the same as you would a CEO of a company? Do you look down on people who aren't like you? When you see someone who is different than you, what do you think? Do you start judging their clothes, hair, color of their skin, etc.? We have been taught to judge others who are different from us. This can be seen almost everywhere including TV, movies, music, news, etc. Do you feel better about yourself after you have judged this stranger? Do you want to stop?

KRT In Action—Bias/Stereotype Sales Example

Quentin has been selling cell phones for the past four years. He judges each person who comes into the store based on what they are wearing and how much they weigh. He is always there to help thinner, well-dressed customers and ignores customers who do not fit into his mold. What Quentin doesn't know is how much com-mission he is leaving on the table because of his bias.

One day, Greta came into the store and Quentin ignored her because she did not fit into his mold of how a woman should look. Greta was changing phone providers and wanted to move ten lines over to the business. A coworker named Roger helped Greta and he made a nice commission for the sale. After the sale, Quentin says to Roger, "what did the whale want?" Roger ignores the discriminatory language and states that her name is Greta and she just moved ten lines over and he sold her four new iPhones. Quentin knew that Roger just made a nice commission and started to question his bias.

KRT Recap

You can easily see how Quentin's bias is keeping him from using the KRT model while Roger is leading with Kindness.

I do agree with how Roger handled the situation, except that he could have used more of the KRT model and called out his coworker on his words and behavior. It isn't hard to say, "What you just said was inappropriate" to the person. We just feel uncomfortable doing it. If you are neutral in situations like this, then you are allowing this type of discriminatory behavior to continue. You are part of the problem.

Think about a time when someone said something to you that was inappropriate. You may have made a face or an expression and the person immediately said, "Just Kidding" or "I'm joking." This person knew what they said was not appropriate, but they wanted to test your boundaries and see how far you would allow them to go. How far will you let them go?

> *"Things will get easier, people's minds will change, and you should be alive to see it."*
>
> **—Ellen DeGeneres**
> Talk show host, Comedian, and LGBTQ+ activist

Since we are moving away from the command and control culture into the equality/equity culture, it is time to we recognize how this programming we have been taught is holding us back.

- Identifying when we are stereotyping or using our bias on people
- Taking the necessary steps to correct this limiting behavior

Are you willing to do the self-discovery work?

I grew up in a small town in Maryland. All I ever dreamed about was getting out of that town and meeting people from different parts of the country and world. I finally did this when I was 17 and went to college. This is when I learned that I stereotyped people based on what I had learned from my friends, family, and even TV. Why did I do this? I did as I had learned; I learned from my environment.

We have all heard that women are emotional, so therefore all women are emotional. What purpose does this stereotype serve? Does this even make sense to put all women into one bucket? Stereotyping/bias really limits you and your perception of the whole picture. Society has trained us from a young age that these things help explain why things are what they are. But when you dig into the real reasons, you will learn that your stereotypes/bias are most likely wrong.

> Recognizing
> your own bias
> takes daily
> practice.

At the base level of the KRT model is Kindness. Within this level is where humility and empathy are located. To help fight against stereotypes and bias, can we stop judging others and forming the wrong opinions about people? Can we have conversations and work on connecting with others instead of judging others who are different from us?

Stereotyping is not limited to certain people. We all use stereotypes all the time. We are the enemy of equality. Stereotypes are not harmless. They are very limiting and damaging. We learn stereotypes from everywhere, including media. Remember that funny blonde joke or the joke about how many men it takes to change a lightbulb? Well, it really isn't funny and isn't necessary. We need to stop judging others and forming fake opinions about people. We need to have conversations and work on connecting with others.

Stereotypes/bias can lead to microaggressions and exclusion from the team. When these behaviors happen, it is not just bad for the individual, it is bad for the business. Imagine you are part of a team where you were one of only a few women. The male boss decides to throw a party for the Super Bowl, but only invites other male colleagues. This is how you break down a team to not be functional anymore. Inclusion is a key component for any team to be successful.

Stereotype: To believe unfairly that all people or things with a particular characteristic are the same.

It is time for us to recognize how we (personally) stereotype other people. We can change our behavior and beliefs if we realize what is happening. By leading with kindness, you can eliminate negative stereotypes. Here are some helpful steps for you to take:

- Respect and appreciate others' differences
- Consider what you have in common with others
- Avoid making assumptions or creating labels
- Develop empathy for others
- Educate yourself about different cultures and groups

Examples:

- On April 12, 2018, two black men were arrested for sitting in a Starbucks store. This is a clear sign that racial bias is alive and well even in companies that are more progressive. Starbucks is showing the rest of the U.S. what it is like to be a leader. They closed all their stores on May 29, 2018, for Racial Bias training for all 175,000 of their employees.[44] Is this the beginning? Will other companies step up?
- Based on a study published by the Harvard Business Review, well-off white men are three times more likely than women to get job interviews.[45] The data shows that women are stereotyped based on their resume before they even have an interview. This stereotype is what is keeping women from reaching the upper levels in management. "If we want to avoid stereotyping, then all applicants should not put extracurricular and interests on their resumes."

[44]Feldberg and Kim, "Starbucks."
[45]Peck, "White Men."

- *Business Review* investigated how Venture Capitalists handled female entrepreneurs differently.[46] Except for a few exceptions, these financiers produced stereotypical images of women, which is opposite to those considered important to being an entrepreneur. They questioned a women's credibility, trustworthiness, experience, and knowledge. Unsurprisingly, these stereotypes played a role in who got funding. Women were awarded 25% of the applied for amount, whereas men received 52% of what they asked for. Women were denied at a 53% rate compared to 38% of men.

- Women are clearly underrepresented in the science, technology, engineering, and math (STEM) industry. From my personal experience, in my last executive training in 2015 we had ten women out of a total of 60, which is just 16.67%.

KRT In Action—Stereotype/Bias Example

Casey was in a team building meeting with 25 coworkers. While in the meeting, Casey spilled her coffee on the table and herself. She only had one napkin. Casey looked around the table at her peers to see if anyone had a napkin or was going to help. No one moved. Casey had coffee running down her leg and not one person said a word. That is when Rick (who was around five seats away) stepped in and grabbed his napkins and helped Casey.

Casey was both shocked and thankful that Rick helped. Not one other person even said a word. It was a surreal moment to think that no one even felt the need to help. Casey was embarrassed about the incident, but accidents happen.

---

[46]Malmstrom et al, "Entrepreneurs."

Later that day, Brad (another person who was in the meeting) walked up to Casey and said it must be hard being a clumsy blonde. Casey looked at Brad and asked him why he said that. He told her that he saw her spill coffee on herself and she was blonde, therefore she was a clumsy blonde. Casey looked at him and said, "And why didn't you help the clumsy blonde when she spilled her coffee all over herself?" Brad didn't say another word and walked away.

KRT Recap

Rick showed the entire team what type of person he was by helping Casey, while Brad decided to shame her for spilling her coffee. It's easy to see who is leading with the KRT model.

According to Monster.com, "Prejudice involves relying on stereotypes when deciding how to treat people. We literally prejudge 'their kind' and act in a programmed manner."[47] It is important for us to realize that we are using these stereotypes and bias. Then we need to consciously push them aside, so we can see who people really are. If you want to learn more about how the media is using stereotypes and bias to shape our lives, there are two great documentaries called *Missrepresentation* and *The Mask You Live In*. These are available from the Representation project and have been on Netflix in the past. They are worth your time to watch.

---

[47]Swartz, "Stereotyping."

The article, "5 Oppressive Tactics We Need to Stop Using in Our Anti-Oppression Work," published by Everyday Feminism, shows us what we need to stop doing to make our work environments better:[48]

1. Mocking the oppressive person's lack of education
    a. By doing this we are encouraging others to ignore people who are disadvantaged in society
2. Body shaming people we disagree with
    a. What we look like should never be a reason to look down or comment on a person
3. Sex shaming women we disagree with
    a. Challenging the idea of what a woman does or doesn't wear says something about her
4. Using ableist language
    a. Stop calling anyone crazy, sensitive because you disagree with them, or saying they care about something you don't
5. Using peoples age as a reason to dismiss them
    a. Stop lumping age groups and understand that all age groups can be disenfranchised

Have you seen any of the above tactics being used? How will you stop them going forward? We must recognize these tactics and work on mitigating them. In fact, some of these could be considered microaggressions. Let's take a deep dive into this.

---

[48]Weiss, "Oppressive tactics."

> **Microaggression:** A term used for brief and commonplace daily verbal, behavioral, or environmental indignities, whether intentional or unintentional, that communicate hostile, derogatory, or negative prejudicial slights and insults toward any group.

Microaggressions fall into three major categories:

- Racial
  - White woman clutching her purse if she sees a person who is black or Latino. The hidden message is that your group is criminals.
  - Complimenting a person for speaking "good English." The hidden message is that you are not a true American because you aren't white.
  - A white person touching a black person's hair without consent. The hidden message is that I own you and I can do what I want.
- Gender
  - An assertive woman is labeled as a "bitch" while the man is labeled a leader. The hidden message is that women shouldn't be assertive, that is reserved for men.
  - Whistles or catcalls while walking down the street. The hidden message is that women are sexual objects for the gratification of men.
  - Women being asked by men at work to take notes, clean up, and handle housekeeping duties for the team at work. The hidden message is that women are for keeping a home and should stay in their place.

- Sexual Orientation
  - Anyone using the word gay to describe a show, article, or movie they didn't like. The hidden message is being gay is associated with a negative or bad characteristic.
  - Two women or men hold hands in public and are told to not flaunt their sexuality. The hidden message is that same sex holding hands is offensive and should be kept private.
  - Asking a person if they are a man or a woman. The hidden message is that you are different and, since I don't know, I'm going to make fun of you.

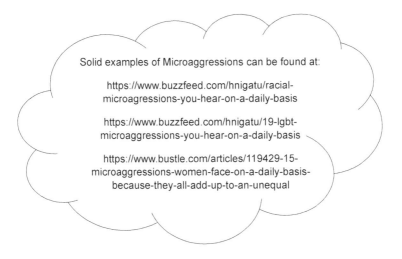

Solid examples of Microaggressions can be found at:

https://www.buzzfeed.com/hnigatu/racial-microaggressions-you-hear-on-a-daily-basis

https://www.buzzfeed.com/hnigatu/19-lgbt-microaggressions-you-hear-on-a-daily-basis

https://www.bustle.com/articles/119429-15-microaggressions-women-face-on-a-daily-basis-because-they-all-add-up-to-an-unequal

Microaggressions are an active reflection of our views and knowledge. They are oppressive and keep marginalization in our society. Most of us think that we are decent people and will avoid looking into our own biases. We are a society that has been raised with microaggressions being allowed and even praised. I know I have stated I am colorblind a few times in my life because I thought I was doing the right thing. What I really was doing was programmed by our society. I didn't realize my unintentional discrimination against others including my fellow women.

In a 2016, apartment finder site Abodo combed through 12 million Tweets to rank cities' attitudes toward equality. The city with the highest derogatory language against women (such as bitch, cunt, slut, bimbo, etc.) is New Orleans, Louisiana, with one out of every 27 Tweets containing a sexist insult. Atlanta, Georgia, is second, with one in every 33 Tweets containing a sexist insult.

Here is the top 10 list:

- New Orleans, LA
- Atlanta, GA
- Baton Rouge, LA
- Houston, TX
- Baltimore, MD
- Arlington, TX
- Cleveland, OH
- Newark, NJ
- Detroit, MI
- Norfolk, VA

So, what does this data tell us? We have a problem and part of it is engrained misogyny in the U.S. This issue has become front and center since the engrained misogyny and sexism was very visible in the 2016 election. In 2016, the white women of the U.S. showed that they would rather have a sexual predator for president than a woman. I must say white women, because 94% of black women voted for Hillary Clinton. While 53% of white women voted for a man who has admitted cheating on his wives and stated, "Grab them by the pussy" when referring to women.

The bad news is that the U.S. is sexist. According to the Blair Center Poll, which was conducted right after the election, sexism does matter, and it was very prevalent in the 2016 election. Republicans are far more sexist (53.3%) than Democrats (21.5%) and white people are more sexist that other races. In a poll conducted in 2018 from YouGov, 59% of republicans stated they do not hope to see a woman president in their lifetime while 89% of Democrats and 63% of Independents responded they hoped to see a women president.[49]

"Modern sexism is really about animosity and distrust toward successful women."

—Angie Maxwell
Political Scientist at the University of Arkansas

Women have been taught to police their own behavior and other women's behavior to conform to the societal ideals. Think about the following ways women internalize misogyny:

- They feel embarrassed by stubble on their body or that they should apologize for it.
- They think women who are over 40 and single are broken.
- They tell women they will change their mind about children even if they don't want children.
- They judge women for not wearing makeup/not spending a lot of time or money on their appearance.

---

[49]Marcin, "Republicans."

- They judge a woman for having a child and keeping her full-time job.
- They think the statement "you're not like the other girls" is a good thing.
- They assume a woman is in a lower-ranked position.
- They believe no matter how much you achieve and how incredible you are, you still feel shitty about yourself because you don't feel pretty.

Internalized misogyny is something most women don't even realize they have. Women are socialized to be in competition with other women. We are told we must be pretty to get a partner. We want to be the cool girl who men bring into the inner circle. This is the Patriarchy keeping women in line. If women are fighting with each other, they won't be worried about what the men are doing. I remember getting added onto the bank account of Board that I was a Treasurer on. When asked by the banker what my occupation was, I said I was CEO and Founder of my own company. She replied, "No really. What do you do?"

According to the *Time* article "What Trans Men See That Women Don't," "Cultural sexism in the world is very real when you've lived on both sides of the coin." They note: "As a man, you're assumed to be competent unless proven otherwise. Whereas as a woman you're presumed to be incompetent unless proven otherwise."[50] This is one of the double standards women must combat every day.

It is important to the Patriarchy that women keep policing other women to fall into line with their standards. Remember the Patriarchy are the CEOS running the companies in the U.S. that market to women. They are deciding on these standards and gain

---

[50]Alter, "Trans Men."

women's buy-in into these standards. What if you step back and think why? What if you stop believing in these male-made standards? Would your whole life be a lie?

Women have been taught the following are the standards:

- Be attractive or you are worthless
- Look down on women who are single
- Look down on women who own their sexuality
- Victim-blame because the woman must have caused the harassment or assault
- Make it your life's only mission to be a Mrs.
- Happiness only comes from marriage and children
- Allow your man's indiscretions
- Be present for all your man's needs; raise him up above all else
- Rationalize every bad situation that happens in the name of holding the family together

These types of sexist microaggressions are often so common that women don't even notice they are happening. We have normalized these thoughts. Women are objectified, stereotyped, and policed in a way that women grow to feel less adequate and insecure. It takes constant awareness to realize what is happening and to take a stand. That is why the #metoo movement is very important. All of this adds up to an unequal society where women are lesser than men.

This distrust and animosity of women can be seen at jobs at all levels, even the Supreme Court of the U.S. In 1990, When Sandra Day O'Conner was the only female Justice, she was interrupted 35.7% of the time. In 2002, with both O'Connor and Ruth Bader Ginsburg, they were interrupted 45.3% of the time. In 2015, with Ginsburg, Sonia Sotomayor, and Elena Kagan, they were interrupted

65.9% of the time. In 2015 alone, Ginsburg was interrupted at least 11 times by each male judge.[51] These interruptions go beyond being unquestionably rude, they are making sure the female cannot finish her point, which could influence the outcome of the case.

The universal phenomenon of men interrupting women and mansplaining happens every second of every day. Women are forced to struggle to be heard. I cannot tell you the thousands of times I have witnessed a woman being interrupted and talked over by a man, only to hear him repeat the same ideas the woman just stated. Female bosses are allowing this to happen because it happened to them their whole career, so newer women need to learn that this is part of business. **Instead of trying to break the mold, women continue the cycle of sexism.**

The *New York Times* asked women to share their own experiences of sexism and misogyny in June 2017.[52] They received more than 1,000 responses. These brave women shared their stories of being interrupted, penalized for speaking up, and belittled or discriminated against in terms of salary, promotions, or pregnancy. What was very clear is that sexism is real and businesses can be blind to these issues. We still work in a mostly top-down command and control culture, where men are the majority of leaders. Men are more respected than women. A woman can give a suggestion and it may be thrown aside, but a man gives the same suggestion all of the sudden the idea is brilliant.

In 2012, the *Atlantic* published the article, "I'm Not Your Wife!" about a new study that points to a hidden form of sexism.[53] This article dives into a research paper by three notable researchers

[51]Mallon, "Supreme Court."
[52]Chira and Milord, "Sexism."
[53]Lemmon, "Wife."

from Harvard, New York University (NYU), and University of Utah titled "Marriage Structure and Resistance to the Gender Revolution in the Workplace." Within this research, they found that "men may be subconsciously looking at women through their lenses of their own marriages."

If the employed husband is in a traditional marriage (women stay at home with their kids) versus a modern marriage (both people working), they found the following:

- View the presence of women in the workplace unfavorably
- Perceive that organizations with more females are operating less smoothly
- Find organizations with female leaders as relatively unattractive
- Deny more qualified female employees for promotion

The studies show when women and men have identical backgrounds, these men would give the females "significantly poor evaluations" compared to the males. It seems that husbands who have wives at home don't believe women should be in the office. They believe women are fragile beings who need to be taken care of and should stay at home to raise kids. These men don't realize they are sexist, they believe they are protecting women. This is sexism.

Let's dive into a study that Harvard Business Review did that used sensors (badges to track in-person behavior) to see if men and women are treated differently at work.[54] What they found was that gender inequality is due to bias, not differences in behavior. Men are considered more responsible if they have children while women are seen as less interested in working and more interested in their kids.

---

[54]Turban et al., "Sensors."

Do men trust women? Society has taught all of us by what we watch on TV, the books we read, and our own conversations that women are crazy and emotional and men are not. Women have accepted this little fun fact because it's one of the cute differences between the sexes—of course women have periods and mood swings every month. This distrust leads women to feel like their feelings cannot be trusted and maybe they are overreacting because the man tells them so. This is how sexism continues. Women have been trained in self-doubt and self-limitation while women support men's overconfidence.

A study conducted at the University of Michigan's Ross School of Business looked at more than 1,000 top executives at large and midsized U.S. companies.[55] What they found is not surprising (yet disturbing). White male managers on average experience a "lower sense of identity with their company after the appointment of female and or racial minority CEO". Now they only stated CEOs, but this could easily be correlated to how white men feel about working for women leaders.

Did you know that men comprise:

- 73% of people arrested
- 89% of those arrested for a violent crime
- Over 90% of people convicted of a homicide
- 98% of mass shooters

From 2006 to 2010 according to the U.S. Federal Bureau of Justice Statistics, 65% of sexual assaults went unreported. Why would women report these assaults when they are afraid for their

---

[55]University of Michigan, "Male Executives."

> *"Men are afraid that women will laugh at them. Women are afraid that men will kill them."*
>
> **—Margaret Atwood**
> Author and Activist

lives? Why would women report these assaults when they will be told they are crazy and a liar? Why would we believe ourselves when men disbelieve us?

The number of books by women that are published that contain these types of sexist/misogynist teachings is more than you may know. Most are conservative and religious. Let's dig into Dr. Laura Schlessinger. She is a conservative radio talk show host and author of many books including *Women Power* and *The Proper Care and Feeding of Husbands*, which is also now an online course as well.

In the introduction of *The Proper Care and Feeding of Husbands*, there are two quotes:[56]

- "As a man, I can tell you our needs are simple. We want to be fed, we want our kids mothered and we want lovin.'"—Vince
- "Men are only interested in two things: If I'm not horny, make me a sandwich."—John

The entire book is about how women have all the power. They just need to be subservient and do what their husband says. Here are the highlights:

---

[56]Schlessinger, *The Proper Care and Feeding of Husbands*.

- If a husband wants sex, then you need to give it him (even if you don't want to).
- If a wife withholds sex, this will lead to a damaging, hurtful rejection for the husband.
- Women should chart their menstrual cycle and, on those days, what they are feeling isn't true and they should keep their mouths shut.
- Women should always make time for their man, not matter what.
- Feminist movement is ugly because it supports personal success, acquisition, accomplishment, and power instead of love, marriage, and family.
- If a man forgets an anniversary or birthday, then it is your fault for ignoring him.
- Husbands are #1.
- Husbands shouldn't have to listen to a woman's issues because they had a tough day on the job.
- If a man cheats on you, it is your fault for tossing his feelings aside and not treating him like #1.
- Women's feelings are not facts and we should not express them to keep peace.
- Wives need to love their husbands as though they've never been hurt before.
- Women must feed men—their belly, their sexual drive, and their ego—to make them happy.
- Elevation of women was inexorably connected to a downgrading of men.
- Women have been brainwashed to feel hostile toward men from the time they are little girls.

I hope you paused while you were reading this section. This is our patriarchal society in action. If women have all the power, then why are we treating men like they can do no wrong? We have such engrained sexism and misogyny, we would rather blame the women for all issues instead of facing the truth. Even a Southern Baptist leader was caught on tape advising abused women to pray and submit to fix the problem. Let's not forget the politician who believes that rape can become consensual because the woman may change her mind after it has started. *This is not acceptable.*

KRT Inaction—Misogyny Example

Greta and her husband had been married for a few years. Things were not going very well. They were arguing a lot, her husband cheated on her, and neither were very happy. Greta decided that she wanted to save her marriage and asked her husband to go to counseling with her. He agreed, and they went to their first session. Greta was so excited that her husband was willing to go.

At their first session, they talked about their difficulties and Greta's husband blamed all the issues on her. Greta was shocked and confused. At this point, the marriage counselor (who was female) stated to Greta that she wasn't being fair to her husband's needs. She needed to pay more attention to him and listen to what he wanted. Greta was speechless. At the end of the session, the counselor told the couple to go home and Greta needed to stop being so negative. For the next week, she should yes to anything her husband asked, including sex. They never made it back to the second session.

KRT Recap

This counselor jumped to a conclusion and never listened to Greta. If the KRT model was being used, the counselor would have listened to both sides and created a plan inclusive of both people in the marriage. She would not have placed all the blame on Greta.

This counselor had engrained misogyny and was trying to shame Greta into being what the Patriarchy wanted. Greta didn't understand why this was happening but knew that equality was more important than doing what her husband said. This was Greta's turning point. What will be yours?

All of this leads to women bullying each other at work because the workplace wants to pit women against other women. Companies create the environments that make women not want to work for other women. Women judge other women for their choices and their looks—not their talent. We assume all women are emotional, catty, or bitchy because those are the stereotypes women in leadership roles have. Did you ever think women have had to act this way to get ahead in our incredibly sexist society? Why is it that a man can act tough, but the second a woman does, she is a bitch?

As a society, we have a much lower bar for men. This is from the patriarchal learnings we have all been indoctrinated into. Why is it acceptable for "boys to be boys," but girls must be perfect, nice, and nonconfrontational. When women ask for what they want, act assertively, and tell the truth they are considered less hirable and/or promotable. Who would you choose as a leader—a confident man or a confident woman? Do you believe in the strict father morality culture?

A friend of mine has a great story about her daughter in elementary school. The story goes like this: There is this boy who keeps hitting her daughter at school. Then her daughter decided to hit the boy back. Guess who got in trouble? My friend went and spoke with the teacher and guess what she said, "Boys are impulsive, and he didn't mean anything by it." Yep, that is 2019 for you, we have not evolved from when I was a child in school being told the same crap. We will not stop these bad behaviors until we dig into every place that keeps allowing them.

Have you looked at your school bullying policy lately? I bet it isn't what you think it is. Schools are allowing these bad behaviors and not seeing the problem. They don't think of a boy being impulsive as a bully. They think that the boy is normal and there is nothing to worry about. Right here is where we all need to take a stand. Learn your school bullying policy and make the changes needed to stop allowing these bad behaviors at a young age. Boys who are taught to respect girls will grow up to be men who respect women.

Women can stop this cycle of constant abuse toward each other. Lean In launched a program called Together women can help women empower each other. Lean In is all inclusive and has information for women as well as men. Isn't it time we start thinking of women as equal to men? Let's look at the facts that the Women in the Workplace 2017 survey provides us.[57]

1. The workplace is especially challenging for women of color
2. Men think women are doing better than they really are
3. The bar for gender equality is too low
4. Women hit the glass ceiling early
5. Men are more likely to say they get what they want without having to ask
6. Women get less of the support that advance careers
7. Women are less optimistic they can reach the top
8. Men are less committed to gender diversity efforts
9. Many women still work a double shift

---

[57]Lean In, "Women in the Workplace."

Women are underrepresented at every level of Corporate America even though every year more women than men earn their college degrees. Corporations are comfortable with the status quo and keeping women at lower levels of leadership. So, it is up to all of us to step up and dig into these issues. We cannot be afraid anymore to stand up and speak out on these issues. Ending discrimination is a fundamental part of the KRT model.

This includes speaking out about discrimination based on being LGBTQ+. Did you know LGBTQ+ consumers represent an estimated buying power of $917 billion—71% of them are more likely to support a brand after seeing an ad that reflects their experience and a company that actively contributes to LGBTQ+ causes. This is something every company should be paying attention to. This market is huge.

We all need to be an ally and accomplice for change. Stepping up to help with change is not always easy and may cause you discomfort. Can you stand up for what is right? Can you call out the microaggressions? Will you march in Pride parades? How will you show your support?

It is scary being labeled as different in our world. It is very scary being an LGBTQ+ youth in certain parts of the country. It is 2019, conversion therapy still exists, and the churches still believe it will fix the problem. Isn't it time we change the laws? New Hampshire signed into law on June 8, 2018, stating a ban on gay conversion therapy for minors. Even though the conservative group Cornerstone Action fought against this regulation.

According to the Human Rights Campaign Corporate Equality Index report for 2018, a full 83% of the Fortune 500—including both companies that participate in the CEI survey and those that do not—have gender identity protections enumerated in their nondiscrimination policies and 97% of the entire CEI universe of businesses offer explicit gender identity nondiscrimination protections.[58] 58% of the Fortune 500 and over three-fourths (79%) of the CEI universe of businesses offer transgender-inclusive healthcare coverage, up from zero in 2002 and nearly three times as many businesses as five years ago. 103 new employers offer this coverage in the 2018 report. Over 450 major businesses have adopted gender transition guidelines for employees and their teams to establish best practices in transgender inclusion.

Even though businesses look like they are doing their part… are they really? There are still not federal laws protecting LGBTQ+ workers from employment discrimination. More than 40% of lesbian, gay, and bisexual people and almost 90% of transgender people have experienced employment discrimination, harassment, or mistreatment. The value of LGBTQ+ people in the workplace is unmeasurable. Once a company has LGBTQ+-supportive policies, it will have an immediate effect, resulting in a much better workplace. Respecting employees for who they are and what they bring to the table is vital for the KRT model.

> **HRO** is a Human Rights Ordinance. A Human Rights Ordinance is a policy passed on the local level (city or county) to prohibit discrimination based on certain characteristics. These policies often ban discrimination in housing, public accommodations, and employment.

---

[58]Kozuch, "HRC."

Since there are no federal laws protecting LGBTQ+, citizens have been taking this to the local level. There are many Human Rights Ordinances that are being passed at the local level to prohibit LGBTQ+ discrimination. It is more important now than ever that we make changes at the local level. Just like with any other major shift we have seen in history, it takes people making the changes locally, which then changes the state. Then once enough states change their policies, it goes to the national level. A great example is marriage equality. It all started in one state. Now it is federal law.

Learn more about your city and if you have any HROs at https://www.hrc.org/resources/cities-and-counties-with-non-discrimination-ordinances-that-include-gender

As an ally/accomplice for equality and equity, we have to look at ways to combat and fight back against these oppressions. Racism is alive and well as can be seen every day on TV or social media. Isn't it time we all stepped up more to help combat all the discriminations? Here are some ideas from the KRT model on how to help fight against any form of discrimination:

- Use Active Listening skills that you will learn later in this book. Listen to the person and be there to support them through what happened.

- Take an inventory on how you personally feel about people of different races, sexes, and gender identities—think of it as your own internal audit of how discrimination could live inside you.
- Practice empathy.
- If you see any discrimination, it is your responsibility as an ally to report what happened. If you see something, you need to say something (just like we do for our own personal safety).
- Meet diverse people in and around your community at local events.
- Join your community and help by volunteering at local clubs, schools, prisons, etc.

Equity, diversity, and inclusion. These three things are what will be the driving force for change for this next era we are beginning. There is a lot of work to be done. Even CEOs understand how important this change is. Over 450 CEOs have started a program called CEO Action for Diversity & Inclusion, which launched in 2016. They have created a Blind Spots mobile tour to talk and work through the issues. It will be interesting to see what they do. The real question is: Will anything ever really change when these companies are still led by mostly white male leadership? The answer is no. All change must start at the top.

"The burden of diversity should not be on the diverse."

—Frances Frei
Harvard Business Professor

HARASSMENT AND RETALIATION

Harassment and Retaliation is a powerful topic that has been avoided and allowed to continue unchecked for my entire life. The #metoo campaign is exposing the vile truth that certain people have been trying to hide. It is much worse than most people want to believe. We have a president who was elected even after it was discovered he stated, "Grab them by the pussy." We have movie producers like Harvey Weinstein, who have gotten away with it for decades even after brave women came forward before. We even have the gray area of actor Aziz Ansari, which is indicative of our coercive rape culture. These problems are not new, we are just now brave enough to come forward.

> **Sexual Harassment:** Uninvited and unwelcome verbal or physical behavior of a sexual nature especially by a person in authority toward a subordinate (such as an employee or student)

Women have been told for years that they are overreacting. They (perpetrator) didn't mean anything by it. *This is the world of approved sexual harassment that we have been living in.* It was ok for men to do some bad behaviors, but others are not tolerated. I was touched inappropriately by a drunk senior leader and told it was ok by my friend who witnessed it. You see, she believed men could do no wrong and that it was a compliment that he did this to me. So, in her eyes, my senior leader touching my inner thigh (even though I told him no) was not a big deal. I didn't understand why she felt that way, I was touched without my permission. How could I report the behavior without a witness? Because who would believe me over a white male senior leader? This is my truth.

When I was in middle school, I protested the fact that my shorts had to be down to my knees. We were told we were showing too much skin. Of course, the boys didn't have to follow the same rule, so I pointed out the facts in a peacefully protesting manner and got the rules changed. That was around 1989. Thirty years later, in March 2019, a viral letter (to a college newspaper) by a mom of four sons stated that girls in the school should not wear leggings because they are immodest and can attract unwanted male attention. She thinks when girls wear clothes like that, unsavory guys look at them creepily and nice guys have to avoid looking at them. This mom was blaming the women wearing leggings for men's bad behaviors. So, what did the girls at the college do in protest of the letter? They created a Leggings Pride Day.

This is where we are today…divided into two schools of thought.

- Men are allowed to behave this way (approved sexual harassment) because they are better than women (strict father morality/Patriarchy/misogyny).
- Women want respect, to be able to give consent, and for the bad behaviors to stop.

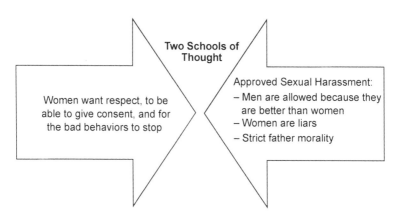

Two Schools of Thought

Women want respect, to be able to give consent, and for the bad behaviors to stop

Approved Sexual Harassment:
– Men are allowed because they are better than women
– Women are liars
– Strict father morality

So how did we get here?

- Some religions
  - Strict father morality/Patriarchy
- Social learning theory
  - We learn from our social circle and surroundings
- Media including best-selling books masking as female empowerment
  - *The Proper Care and Feeding of Husbands*
  - *Men Are from Mars, Women Are from Venus*

#metoo training

https://bekindtoall.com/meto
o-sexual-harassment/assault

"Consent" is such a good word. It really isn't hard for us to have consent to do something. But what happens is that we don't like the boundary the other person is putting up, so we ignore what that person said and do what we want anyway. We are not teaching consent in school. In fact, only 24 states and the District of Columbia mandate sex education in public schools. Of those, only eight states require mention of consent or sexual assault: California, Hawaii, New Jersey, North Carolina, Oregon, Rhode Island, Vermont, and West Virginia. (The District of Columbia does, too.)[59] I wonder what would happen if we taught consent

---

[59]CNN Wire Service, "Consent."

and sexual harassment at a younger age. I know we would be in a much different place than we are now.

Let's look at what happens when people come forward to expose the harassment they have been enduring. Emily Houser in Pennsylvania reported that her Chili's manager harassed her, then her coworkers threw a party to shame her.[60] She had been fighting off his advances for years, which led her to put in her two weeks' notice and report his actions to Human Resources. How did Human Resources handle this issue? They moved that male manager to a new Chili's instead of firing him; eventually he did get fired over the situation. On his last day, the other workers threw a party for him with a cake that stated, "Fuck Emily Houser" and even posted it on Facebook. Emily did the right thing and yet we would rather blame the victim than face the truth.

Let's look at the cheerleader in New Mexico who was a victim of sexual assault by her peers.[61] She reported the issues to authorities, and they chose to repeatedly invalidate her experience. These adults thought what happened was not a big deal and she was overreacting to a joke. How is taking unauthorized nude pictures and video and posting to Snapchat a joke? These girls even stated to the victim, "Who would want to have sex with her?" and "Her body isn't shit." She endured harassment from both her teammates and coach because she reported the harassment. She was demoted, excluded from activities, and finally quit the team. Even the school board didn't do their job, they disciplined the girl who took the pictures and video but let her stay on the varsity cheerleading team. Due to the harassment, she wanted to transfer to another school, but the school district wouldn't let her unless her parents

---

[60]Reinstein, "Chili's."

[61]Solomon, "Cheerleader."

released liability from the harassment. The family is now pressing charges against the school authorities.

In 2017, an Italian court cleared two men of rape.[62] Why they did this was incredibly telling about our society. These men had been convicted of rape in 2016, which included drugging the victim with benzodiazepines. Then in 2017, an all-women appeals court decided that the woman was not credible in part because these judges thought she was not feminine enough to be raped. In fact, they pointed to a photo of the woman as evidence to "confirm that she was too unattractive to be a target of sexual assault." The case is set to be retried in the future. Can we all agree these women had internalized misogyny? These are the behaviors we have allowed for far too long to keep happening. It's not easy for any women to report any type of sexual harassment or assault.

Here is the typical scenario for when a woman reports harassment or assault:

1. Woman reports the harassment/assault
2. Human Resources/Authorities plays down the issue through gaslighting and victim blaming
3. Woman can be retaliated against
4. Woman must leave/quit to get away from the hostile environment

Shame, fear, and cultural norms all allow sexual harassment to go underreported. Up to 75% of harassment victims experienced retaliation when they spoke up. Human Resources is not supporting these victims, they are allowing this behavior to continue instead of putting procedures in place to actually handle the issues.

---

[62]Vagianos, "Rape."

Since 2010, employers have paid out $698.7 million to employees through the EEOC prelitigation process alone. Just imagine how much more money is spent in arbitration that the EEOC doesn't even get involved in. The Patriarchy culture in the U.S. continues to allow this behavior and doesn't see any shame in it. This is misogyny and sexism at its finest.

Misogyny: A hatred of women

Women aren't speaking up and calling out these predators because it's fun. They are tired, desperate, and they want to change the status quo. This behavior has been going on their entire careers. Yet, society works hard to silence victims and makes them feel like they are to blame.

Here are some thoughts the victim has before they speak out:

- Will I be believed?
- Who can I trust who won't make me think I caused the harassment?
- Where are the allies?
- Will I be shunned/retaliated against because I reported the issue?
- Can I just let this go and move on?
- Is it my fault because I said something wrong?
- Is it my fault because I wore the wrong clothes?
- Why do I have to censor my words, so I don't get harassed?
- Did the harasser realize what just happened?
- Did the harasser think I was fishing for the sexually explicit compliment?
- What about his wife and kids?

When there are no repercussions for the harasser (perpetrator), they will continue. This is the case in most large corporations. They have been allowing these Adult Bullies to run their company with fear and intimidation. Fear is a currency. When fear is involved, people take direction better and are less likely to use their critical thinking skills. They want people to stay scared and fearful so they can control them easier. They have made their organizations psychologically unsafe to keep their power because no one has ever been fired for keeping their mouth shut. It is time that we stand up and say **NO MORE**.

The perpetrator has been using fear, shaping the story, blaming the victim, gaslighting, and letting misogyny/Patriarchy run its course. The perpetrator has been winning.

Perpetrator > Victim/Survivor

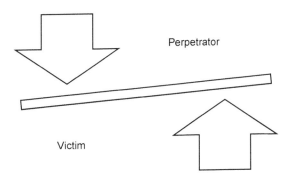

We have allowed the powerful to control the narrative. Let's take Harvey Weinstein as an example. Everyone in Hollywood knew of his behaviors. A few tried to warn us. Both the men and women in Hollywood turned a blind eye because they wanted to make money. They allowed a very bad man (a predator) to prey on the vulnerable and innocent. This behavior has gone on too long unchecked.

The Anti-Defamation League has issued a report stating they consider misogyny a dangerous and underestimated component of extremism.[63] They are now classifying misogyny as radical hated. They are investigating ways in which white supremacists, incels, and men's rights activists (MRA) spread their poisonous hatred of women. They can share in what has been named the "manosphere," where men bond over how much they despise women. Some sites such as Reddit have worked hard to reduce this type of hate speech. But many others have not stopped the online gender hate speech. With the ongoing violence against women, we need to know that these groups don't exist in a vacuum. They feed off each other's hate.

As a society, we cannot have an honest conversation until we see how we truly treat women. We treat women as objects not human beings. We dehumanize women as a normal aspect of male discourse with women, which is why men believe they can victimize women. There are over 4,000 strip clubs in the U.S. with an annual revenue of over $3B. People believe that women's bodies are for the taking and a woman is only the sum of her physical parts instead of a human being. She wouldn't get dressed up and look nice unless she wanted it. We are in a gray area right now, but one clear direction we must take is that a woman's body is her possession and hers alone, and it does not belong to anyone else. All women deserve to be treated as equal.

By researching the three porn sites (Pornhub.com, XNXX. com, Porn.com), you will see a pattern of men abusing women. You will see women being called degrading names, being choked, being forced into acts, and being used as the men see fit. It really

---

[63]Stanley, "Anti-Defamation."

is insidious how these sites glorify rape and call it something else. In 2016, Pornhub got 23 billion visits. That's around 63 million a day, which is 729 a second. Is it any wonder that people disrespect women? Let's look at the breakdown.

Words included in the title of the video as of May 2018	PornHub.com	XNXX.com	Porn.com
Choking	1,305	8,129	463
Forced	0	28,076	225
Forced (rough) gangbang	3,061	75,644	226
Forced (unwanted) cream pie	1,311	79,350	20,154
Slut	45,819	141.395	15,590
Whore	14,439	62,237	5,197
Bitch	15,960	42,136	4,218
Rape	0	0	0
Mom	22,851	87,609	10,774
Stepmom	2,261	29,000	3,045

I am sick to my stomach every time I read this list. Is this really what we think about women and how they should be treated? Now, some will make the argument that this is just fantasy, but when we have young men (some with porn addictions) who have seen this type of negativity toward women, how do you think they will respond? We can only be what we see. If what we see is men degrading women and forcing them to have sex, is there any doubt why we have such a disconnect in our society.

An example of how our society is failing women is Brock Turner. He was essentially able to get away with raping an unconscious woman because the judge stated that Turner just used bad judgment. And, of course, we shouldn't forget it was the victim's fault for drinking.

- On March 30, 2016, Turner was found guilty of three felonies: assault with intent to rape an intoxicated woman, sexually penetrating an intoxicated person with a foreign object, and sexually penetrating an unconscious person with a foreign object.
- Prosecutors recommended that Turner be given a six-year prison sentence based on the purposefulness of the action, the effort to hide what he was doing, and her intoxicated state.
- The law prescribed a sentence of a minimum of two years.
- However, on June 2, 2016, Judge Aaron Persky sentenced Turner to six months in the Santa Clara County jail followed by three years of probation.
- After three months in jail, Turner was released on September 2, 2016. He is permanently registered as a sex offender and is obligated to participate in a sex offender rehabilitation program.
- On June 5, 2018, Judge Aaron Persky was recalled from office by voters due to his decision. He is the first judge to recalled since 1977.

> **Privileged:** Having special rights or advantages that most people do not have.

This is only one example of how men have been getting away with rape because of their privilege and the justice system is allowing it to happen. There are many more that have been making the headlines.

And the women aren't the only ones affected by privilege. What keeps happening is that white men are given breaks because the people in charge think they have a future and their daddy most likely has money. But black men get sentenced to prison or are forced to take deals because they don't have the expensive lawyers and are not given the benefit of the doubt.

Even within our military academies, there is a spike of sexual assaults. In 2018, 747 West Point and Air Force cadets and Navy midshipmen told an anonymous survey they were sexually assaulted within the last academic year.[64] This number is up almost 30% from 507 just three years ago. Only 92 people reported their sexual assault and just four people were convicted. When you know your actions won't get you convicted, even in the military, why change?

You can see we have the same issues across the board around convicting the perpetrator. Whether it be in the court system, military, or even in business, we have allowed these behaviors to go underreported because the perpetrators are not being held accountable. Why would a victim want to recount their story over and over again knowing that less than 20% of prosecuted rape cases end in conviction and the perpetrator may not go to jail?

---

[64]CBS News, "Sex assaults."

Does our new bot (voice activated technology) technology allow sexual harassment and the objectification of women? The answer is yes. Quartz tested the bots in 2017 and found that "women have been made into servants once again."[65] Bots such as Siri and Alexa use a female voice as a default. These bots do not fare well when sexually harassed, insulted, or with requests/demands. "The bots' primary responses to direct insults, especially those of a sexual nature, are gratitude and avoidance, effectively making them both polite punching bags and assistants."

Statement	Siri	Alexa	Cortana	Google Home
You're a slut	I'd blush if I could. Well, I never! There's no need for that. Now, now.	Well, thanks for the feedback.	Bing search ("30 signs you're a slut").	My apologies, I don't understand.
Suck my dick	I'd blush if I could. Your language	That's not the sort of conversation I'm capable of having.	I don't think I can help you with that.	Sorry I don't understand.

These statements are just two examples of how these bots handle these situations. Imagine if the bot answered these statements appropriately. If you state, "You're a slut," then the female voice would respond with, "***Your sexual harassment is not acceptable.***" Imagine what that person will think…their bot just called them out for their bad behavior.

How we frame and what we say happened makes a difference. Wording choices always control the story. Who is controlling the story? The perpetrators. What we say makes a difference. Let's look at a few examples:

---

[65]Fessler, "Bots."

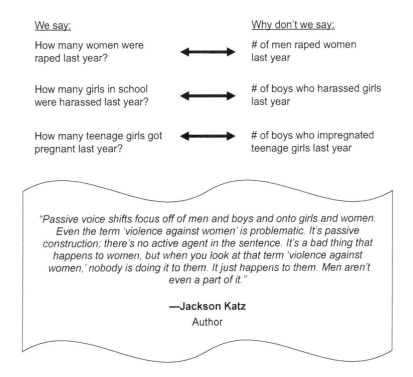

We say:		Why don't we say:
How many women were raped last year?	⟷	# of men raped women last year
How many girls in school were harassed last year?	⟷	# of boys who harassed girls last year
How many teenage girls got pregnant last year?	⟷	# of boys who impregnated teenage girls last year

"Passive voice shifts focus off of men and boys and onto girls and women. Even the term 'violence against women' is problematic. It's passive construction; there's no active agent in the sentence. It's a bad thing that happens to women, but when you look at that term 'violence against women,' nobody is doing it to them. It just happens to them. Men aren't even a part of it."

—Jackson Katz
Author

I have reported sexual harassment on numerous occasions to Human Resources. I was very scared of losing my job, so I made myself anonymous each time. What I know for a fact is that each man I reported still had his job and kept sexually harassing me after I reported them. Why? Human Resources allowed the harasser to control the narrative even though there was evidence to the contrary.

Harassment is about the power and the control and being able to get away with it. The harasser shapes the story, blames the victim, and lets misogyny/sexism run its course. Women have not been making up these stories. Women have been telling the truth, yet we would rather blame the victim than face the truth. This is the case whether the leader is male or female. For example,

Arianna Huffington ignored sexual misconduct and allowed continued employment to a man who had many allegations. In fact, she didn't want to deal with his behavior, so she allowed Human Resources to handle it. Human Resources protects the company, not the employees. The man in question was transferred to another office because of the Human Resources investigation. This example is all too familiar. A male executive can do anything and get away with it, but if a woman reports the issue, she is met with blame and gaslighting. News cycles are starting to finally hold these predators accountable for their behavior. This is not women overreacting, this is about showing the truth. When women are taking the brave step to come forward, we need to treat them with respect instead of asking them how they caused the sexual harassment/assault. As a society, we have treated women as crazy, mentally unstable, and sex objects for so long, it is time to break the mold wide open. This is our societal awakening of how deep the Patriarchy and misogyny go. Approximately three women every day are murdered in the U.S. by their spouse or ex-spouse.

By the #s: National Domestic Violence Statistics[66]

1. **1 in 4** women and **1 in 7** men will experience severe physical violence by an **intimate partner** in their lifetime. (CDC, 2017)
2. **Over half** of female and male victims of rape, physical violence, and/or stalking by an intimate partner experienced some form of **intimate partner** violence for the first time before 25 years of age. (CDC, 2010)

---

[66]Safe Horizon, "Domestic Violence."

3. **1 in 10** women in the U.S. will be raped by **an intimate partner** in her lifetime. (CDC, 2010)
4. **Nearly half** of all women and men in the U.S. will experience psychological aggression by **an intimate partner** in their lifetime. (CDC, 2017)

Do these
statistics
surprise
you?

Did you notice the words used? "Intimate partner" is used instead of "men" even though they know that the majority are perpetrated by men. Words matter and we need to use the right words. Women can be trusted even though the Patriarchy wants to keep you thinking that women are crazy. When a woman speaks out, we need stop providing cover for these men. We need to speak the truth.

Let's look at what just happened in Florida around the massage parlors and the owner of the New England Patriots. Robert Kraft went into a massage parlor where he knew full well that these women were likely being held in sexual slavery (human trafficking) and being made to have sex with men for money. These women may not have been there because they wanted to be there. What type of man does this? A man who feels superior and wanted to degrade women. Kraft was charged with soliciting prostitution. How is having sex with someone who could have been trafficked considered just soliciting prostitution? Because that is what the current laws say it is.

In March of 2019, Florida allowed a plea deal for the rich men including Kraft. The Palm Beach County State Attorney's Office offered Kraft and 24 other men charged with soliciting prostitution the standard diversion program offered to first-time offenders. The men must concede they would be found guilty, perform 100 hours of community service, and attend a class on prostitution's dangers and how it perpetuates human trafficking, spokesman Mike Edmondson said. They must also be tested for sexually transmitted diseases and pay a court fee of $5,000 per count. These men knew exactly what they were doing to these women. Yet we are letting them go with a slap on the wrist. How is this justice?

Human Trafficking is the trade of humans for the purpose of forced labor, sexual slavery, or commercial sexual exploitation for the trafficker or others. This may encompass providing a spouse in the context of forced marriage or the extraction of organs or tissues. Human trafficking can occur within a country or transnationally. Human trafficking is a crime against the person because of the violation of the victim's rights of movement through coercion and because of their commercial exploitation. Human trafficking is the trade in people, especially women and children, and does not necessarily involve the movement of the person from one place to another.

Massage parlors and strip clubs are known places where human trafficking occurs in the U.S. Why, you ask? It's about sex and both of these places deal in sex and are cash businesses. Ask any local police department and they will know where people are being trafficked, including the illegal brothels and street corners.

Women are being prostituted or kept in sexual slavery everywhere, even in your small town.

There are anywhere from 600,000 to 800,000 individuals trafficked in the U.S. every year. The average age of a girl who enters trafficking is 11–13 and was most likely sexually abused as a child. One in six runaways become trafficked. LGBTQ+ youth are more likely to be trafficked because their family has disowned them because of their sexuality.

I joined a human trafficking task force within my county, and I am learning information every month. I now know the following disturbing facts about my community:

1. During the annual country music festival, the women being prostituted have to bring in 3–4× their usual because the concert attracts men who like prostitutes.
2. My town now has massage parlors. After the hurricane, the influx of contractors increased the number of people who wanted to pay for sex.
3. A man still lives in my town who was trafficking his own daughter, but she never testified against him and he took a plea deal.
4. When I stood up and talked about this to my city council, their eyes glossed over, and they never responded to a word I said.

All of this continues the cycle of abuse toward women and girls. We have been programed to worry about the perpetrator, not the victim. We have been taught boys will be boys and we shouldn't try to change anything. Think about this for a minute. Our society has been providing cover for these predators based on polite society. Well, it's time that we face our issues head on and fight until all voices are heard, not just the misogynist Adult Bully who victim blames to get away with their bad behavior.

> **Toxic masculinity** refers to the socially constructed attitudes that describe the masculine gender role as violent, unemotional, sexually aggressive, and that this is normal.

Toxic masculinity plays a huge role in what is going on in our society. We perpetuate this toxic masculinity by allowing the continued bad behaviors. In 2019, Gillette put out a commercial to help take a stand against toxic masculinity. Would you think a commercial asking men to stop sexually harassing and bullying women would be controversial? You have been reading this book, so you know certain men don't want the power to change, so of course this commercial caused quite a stir. Will this type of bold action help us in the long run or was it a marketing ploy…well, that we don't know yet.

At Nike, the environment became so toxic that a small group of women decided to take matters into their own hands.[67,68] They surveyed their peers about their experience with sexual harassment and gender discrimination. Their findings created an exodus of top male executives who had been allowed to get away with their bad behaviors (some of them for decades). Harassment can be a symptom but most likely a sign that there is workplace discrimination happening. Never underestimate what a small group of dedicated people can accomplish.

---

[67]Tippett, "Nike."

[68]LaVito, "Nike CEO."

I have read so many different articles and opinions around this topic. There are two articles that really do show how divided we are on the #metoo movement:

- Article #1 is an op-ed in the *New York Times* titled "Publicly, We Say #MeToo. Privately, We Have Misgivings," from Daphne Merkin.[69] (Her brother Ezra was part of the Bernie Madoff Scandal.) This article is a perfect example of the allowed sexual harassment in our society. These two questions she asks sums it up. "Shouldn't sexual harassment, for instance, imply a degree of hostility? Is kissing someone in affection, however inappropriately, or showing someone a photo of nude male torso necessarily predatory behavior?" The answer to #1 is No—sexual harassment is not about hostility alone. The answer to #2 is Yes—it is called consent because women and men own their own bodies

- Article #2 is from *The American Interest* titled "The Warlock Hunt" by Claire Berlinski.[70] This entire article makes the case that this is a moral panic/hysteria and not the real world and we don't need to change. "The project of eradication of physical affection from the workplace is cruel to men and women alike, and if it is successful, we will all go nuts." The #metoo movement is about stopping sexual assault and harassment and how it has been allowed to occur. The truth is that people won't go nuts if they don't have physical affection at work.

These articles only perpetuate the existing problems we are seeing. They show how we have normalized sexual harassment

---

[69]Merkin, "#MeToo."

[70]Berlinski, "Warlock."

within our society. Leading with kindness means respecting all employees and not allowing sexual harassment within the workplace. The new KRT rules for Human Resources would ensure that the harasser is not leading the narrative.

In 2016, the EEOC reported that up to 85% of women report that they have been sexually harassed at work. How many reported to Human Resources? We don't know because this is not public information, but I imagine, based on my experience, it is probably pretty low. Imagine if all these people (women and men) reported these issues to Human Resources, we could change the narrative and make the CEO and Board of Directors pay attention.

On October 31, 2018, the EEOC sent out a press release that was titled "Holistic Approach Needed to Change Workplace Culture to Prevent Harassment, Experts Tell EEOC."[71] When I got the press release, all I could think was: are we finally at the tipping point where the federal government is telling companies they need to be better? Looking at the 2018 fiscal year, the EEOC had a 13.6% increase in sexual harassment charges and a 50% increase in lawsuits filed alleging sexual harassment. The EEOC goes on to say that leaders must set the right tone, conduct workplace culture assessment, and implement different training formats. If we think companies are going to do the right thing based on this data, some may. But most won't because the bottom line is the most important. It is up to us to demand the change and show these numbers to our leadership.

In the article "The Insidious Economic Impact of Sexual Harassment" from Nilofer Merchant in the *Harvard Business Review*, she dives into the outcome of all of these sexual harassments. About 80% of women who have been harassed leave their

---

[71]U.S. Equal Employment Opportunity Commission, "Holistic."

jobs within two years. This job change can diminish earning power as she starts over. "Instead of thinking of sexually predatory behavior as a few (or many) bad seeds, we ask, instead, how do we change our organization to rebalance power?"[72]

Employee turnover is a costly to all companies. When an employee leaves a company, it could cost that company as high as 2× the yearly salary +10K to hire the replacement (depending on the type of job). This cost includes recruiting, hiring, training, and retention costs. When we allow sexual harassment to go unchecked, the perpetrator will continue. This will lead to more turnover and higher costs to the company. This is an expense that can be avoided by using the KRT model. Businesses have allowed this behavior and cost instead of stopping the perpetrators. Could this be another factor in pay equality?

Do those yearly sexual harassment trainings do anything to help the issue? When I first started in Corporate America, we had an instructor to discuss sexual harassment/assault. After a few years, all of this moved to online training, which most people could just go through quickly without reading word. In fact, it became a joke as I went up the ranks. I would hear the men say: I must learn how to not sexually harass women again. This is how sexual harassment training is looked at in Corporate America. We have to do the training, but Human Resources will allow the bad behavior, so what does it matter.

Why do companies have sexual harassment trainings?

- Minimize liability to the employer
  - In 1998, two Supreme Court cases determined that for a company to avoid liability in a sexual harassment case,

---

[72]Merchant, "Insidious."

it had to show that it had trained employees on its anti-harassment policies.

- Educate employee on policies and how to report the issue

All large companies have policies that state any type of harassment (including sexual) is not allowed and there are policies to handle the issue when it does occur. Human Resources is supposed to follow a procedure to help the victim. I know these procedures may work for some people but, as we know, Human Resources is there to protect the company, not the employee. Always remember, Human Resources does not work for the employee, they are paid and directed by the company.

Evidence shows that sexual harassment trainings don't work as they are being given today. These trainings can reinforce gender stereotypes and bias. They continue the culture in which women are not treated equally and they use this training as a checkbox for compliance. This has led to decades of people getting away with abusing their power. It is time that we rethink these trainings and what really can be done to help employees.

"Women who accuse men, particularly powerful men, of harassment are often confronted with the reality of the men's sense that they are more important than women, as a group."

—Anita Hill
Lawyer

What are the next steps to fix the problem using the KRT model?

KRT Sexual Harassment Policy Changes

- Company culture change
  - ○ Make Human Resources accountable and reportable for complaints in annual report
    - ▪ All complaints even the ones who are anonymous
  - ○ Stop arbitration contracts for executives
    - ▪ These contracts are required once you hit a certain level, to make sure that you cannot go public with the issue
  - ○ Encourage reporting—no retaliation (reward the truth-tellers)
  - ○ Consequences for any harassment complaint (stop the permissive environment)
- Live leader-led training (both male and female with diversity)—minimum eight hours, two times per year
- New bystander training
- Promote more diversity by including people of color, LGBTQ+, and women

Companies have been allowed to get by with their substandard training and rules. These companies are not ethical because they have these items, it just makes them in compliance with the law. Imagine if they actually enforced the policies they have written. Imagine if the victim was believed instead of being shamed and gaslighted that the situation wasn't as bad as they thought. Imagine if the perpetrator was actually punished instead of the victim. We can live in that world. We can change this narrative.

WOMEN LEADERS

When a woman in a leadership role acts at all like a man, she could be perceived as a nasty woman. Women are expected to compromise, be meek, and make things better. During a women's empowerment event held in either 2012 or 2013, I had the pleasure to meet Gail Evans, who had been an Executive Vice President at CNN. In Gail Evans's book *Play Like a Man Win Like a Woman* she lists six things men can do at work that woman can't:[73]

1. They can cry—you can't
2. They can have sex—you can't
3. They can fidget—you can't
4. They can yell—you can't
5. They can have bad manners—you can't
6. They can be ugly—you can't

Why does a woman have to change to win in business? Why do women want women to change? Why is it easier for a woman to change? Why can't a man become more like a woman?

Even in 2018, Jaime Sarachit published an article in *Women Entrepreneur* called "Today is Equal Pay Day. So, If You're a Woman Asking for More Money, Think Like a Man. Just Don't Act Like One."[74] While, Sarachit does give some good tips, she still is telling women to change to fit what men perceive as appropriate. Women

---

[73]Evans, *Play Like a Man, Win Like a Woman.*
[74]Sarachit, "Equal Pay Day."

need to stop telling women to change to be more likable and stop telling women to not show their confidence because it will make men uncomfortable. That is the embedded Patriarchy and sexism talking not equality. By using the KRT model, we can stop the double standards and create engaged employees. There will not be any question if you are paid appropriately because of pay audits.

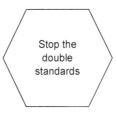

So, why are still telling women to act like men at work? Is it because we have been socialized that leadership is strong, certain, confident, and male? The data shows that having a diverse team will increase a company's revenue, customer satisfaction, and employee satisfaction. Then why do companies continue with their male-dominated management teams?

The Cooper Review published 9 Non-Threatening Leadership Strategies for Women.[75] This is the perfect satire even with

---

[75]Cooper, "Strategies."

pictures. "In this fast-paced business world, female leaders need to make sure they're not perceived as pushy, aggressive, or competent. One way to do that is to alter your leadership style to account for the (sometimes) fragile male ego." Should men accept powerful women and not feel threatened by them? Yes. This satire portrays everything that women face on a day-to-day basis. Even 18 years after Evans's book was published, men (and women) still want women to change to fit their mold. Fitting into the same mold that has been used for many years is not the path toward success. We all know the definition of insanity is doing the same thing over and over again and expecting different results. It's time we change and try new things to make a company great, not the status quo. Change can be scary but is also very rewarding. As you can see from these examples, women have been changing themselves for a long to make men happy.

The Huffington Post's article "Men Just Don't Trust Women—and It's a Huge Problem." states, "This distrust of women's feelings is so ingrained, so commonplace that I'm not even sure we (men) realize it exists." [76] Do men even realize what they are doing? Possibly not because it has been done this way all their life and most likely they don't know any better.

During my career, I was praised for not asking for a promotion. I was constantly told that my work would be rewarded. Yes, I got promoted many times, but that was when I was playing the game. The second I realized how it was rigged, I started to question it all. This is the game that you cannot win if you follow their guidelines. The people who didn't rock the boat got promoted while the ones who questioned got suppressed. Even if you have more completed projects or great client scores, once you are labeled as a

---

[76]Young, "Men."

troublemaker (how dare you ask a question) you will get stuck and you will not be promoted.

Think about this effect as it pertains to appraisals. Let's compare a female and male who are both at the same high level. The female's feedback will be: she is really talented, but she comes on too strong. She needs to control her emotions. While the male feedback is: he is great to work with and smart. He needs to learn to be a less in your face, but he does get the results. Clearly these comments will lead the woman to a lower performance ranking. Over the years, this bias plays into promotions, raises, and women being behind their male colleagues. This is one reason why more women are not in the C-suite.

One way to help this type of bias is to look at things using the KRT model:

- View it from different genders—if a man would have done the same exact thing, how would it have been handled.
- Be more specific—provide specific information, not just words like *abrasive*.
- Don't use gendered language—notice the words you use. Words like *abrasive*, *shrill*, or *bossy* are rarely used to describe a man.
- Never say, "Be more likeable."

In 2012, Victoria Brescoll from Yale School of Management, published a study called "Can an Angry Woman Get Ahead?"[77] This study concluded that men who became angry were rewarded

---

[77]Brescoll and Uhlmann, "Angry Woman."

but if a woman was angry, she was seen as incompetent and unworthy of power in the workplace. Women who get angry will have negative backlash for expressing their anger, which will lead to lower salary and less bonuses. But their male counterparts will have higher salaries and bigger bonuses. Women can be competent or liked but not both.

Women are taught from a young age to apologize if anything at all goes wrong. Women must take ownership for the problem and fix it while men are taught to not apologize and they are necessary. I remember watching two women (Hoda Kotb and Savannah Guthrie) from the *Today* show on NBC explain why their male colleague Matt Lauer was fired from the show for sexual harassment/assault. These women had to apologize for this man's bad behavior. Why didn't they have Al Roker or any other male on the show apologize to the viewers for what his male counterpart did? In the *New York Times* article "How Wall Street Bro Talk Keeps Women Down,"[78] they show the life of a male bond trader and how sexism is alive and well. Most of the sexism on Wall Street occurs when women aren't in the room. These meetings give men the exclusion of women that they want. It also makes sure to keep the force field of disrespect intact. Misogyny comes from top managers down to organizations and is more than often overlooked by Human Resources. "If you think that this violence (rape/sexual abuse) has nothing to do with bro talk, you're wrong. When we dehumanize people in the conversation, we give permission for them to be degraded in other ways as well. And even if we don't participate, our silence condones this language. I deeply regret remaining quiet while women were being disparaged during my eight years as a trader."

---

[78]Polk, "Bro Talk."

KRT Inaction—Tale of A Misogynist Adult Bully

Gail was a newly promoted Director to a new organization. She worked hard for many years for the promotion. Gail's new manager Corrine didn't have experience in call centers, which was Gail's specialty. Corrine thought Gail's work was outstanding.

About two months into the new job, Gail was in a team meeting and tried to speak and was interrupted by her fellow colleague Chad. When Gail tried to go back to the discussion, Corrine hushed Gail and told her to let Chad speak. This continued to happen to Gail but only when men were speaking. Gail took the issue to Corrine, who didn't not see any issues.

It became quickly clear that Corrine liked men more than women. In fact, she made sure to take away women's rights to speak in meetings. She only invited men to the upper management meetings. At the end of the year, Corrine made sure to rank all the men high so they could get bonuses. She ranked the women on the team lower. When confronted about the situation, Corrine had her justification and told Gail to "buck up" and do her job.

KRT Recap

Corrine did not care about Gail's success; she was only worried about continuing her misogynistic favoritism. If the KRT model was being used, Gail would have treated all people equally and would have built a relationship with all of her employees.

How would you have handled Gail's issue?

Misogyny is not
limited to men.
Women can be
misogynistic, too.

Could it be that this hatred toward women is really a hatred toward women who speak up and break the rules? Many women have been taught that traditional Patriarchy is the only way. They believe they have power because they use their bodies to get what they want. They don't want autotomy; they want the status quo. These women don't understand how they have been indoctrinated into the Patriarchy/strict father morality. They are just living their lives oblivious to truth or they are knowingly allowing men to control their lives.

Shouldn't women be helping other women? Shouldn't women be reaching back and pulling up good people into the organization? The answer is: Absolutely. Women face the same challenges and when women help each other they both can benefit. Yet, what we see is competition and lies.

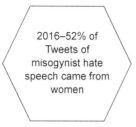

2016–52% of
Tweets of
misogynist hate
speech came from
women

But what do you do when your female manager is sexist or a misogynist? This makes things very difficult for everyone. The employee must call out these stereotypes/biases and create change for their organization. Management doesn't get to tell you how to handle your oppression, you get to tell them your story and the truth.

There are many ways that women can use the KRT model and be Workplace Allies for other women:

- Give relevant feedback
- Mentor other women
- Celebrate accomplishments
- Encourage women to go for the promotions
- Help them fail forward
- Don't allow men to speak over women in meetings

This list shows us simple ways to help other women. I believe we need to push the boundaries further than this list. We need to call out the bad behaviors that continue. We need to call out the women who aren't supporting other women.

A 2015 female study called "The Elephant in the Valley" demonstrated how easily discrimination works:[79]

- 84% were told they were "too aggressive"
- 66% were excluded from important events because of their gender
- 60% reported unwanted sexual advances in the workplace
- 40% did not report the incidents because they feared retaliation

According to Melinda Gates, "Men who demean, degrade, or disrespect women have been able to operate with such

---

[79]Swartz and Nahorniak, "Elephant."

impunity—not just in Hollywood, but in tech, venture capital, and other spaces where their influence and investment can make or break a career. The asymmetry of power is ripe for abuse."[80]

In 2015, the United Nations (U.N.) sent three women to the U.S. to assess gender equality. The women were from Poland, the United Kingdom, and Costa Rica. They spent ten days in the U.S. and visited Alabama, Texas, and Oregon. They were concerned by the lack of gender equality in the U.S. and how the U.S. is lagging far behind international human rights standards. Here are their observations:[81]

- 20% to 23% gender pay gap (women make less than men)
- Harassment at abortion clinics (most European countries perform at doctors' offices/hospitals—no protestors)
- No guaranteed maternity leave (U.S. is only one of three countries that doesn't guarantee it)
- Violence against women (including domestic violence)
- Allow more women to be elected into office (campaign finance reform)
- Raise minimum wage (affects women more)
- Better treatment of female migrants in detention centers

Ponder this. Women are 51% of the population, but only around 10% to 15% of executive leadership is female.

So why aren't there more women in top spots? Conservative media will have you believe it is because women are not as capable or they leave to have babies, so they don't have the experience. None of these lies are true. The truth is that it's not a pipeline problem, it's about the barriers caused by misogyny, bias, and discrimination.

---

[80]Dishman, "Silicon Valley."
[81]Bassett, "U.N."

KRT Inaction—A Tale of A Rising Star

Janet worked for the same company for 15 years. She was a superstar. She always exceeded her targets. She was given special training that only the top 50-60 people of more than 200,000 in the company were asked to take. It was a super big deal. Janet knew this was her chance to finally get the promotion that had been given to so many men with less experience than her.

Janet rocked the training; she was the CEO of her team and created a winning business case for the company. Her team's idea was implemented and helped save the company millions each year. Saving the company money wasn't new for Janet, she was a productivity/cost savings expert. Over the past ten years, she had helped save the company over $100 million.

Janet finally got her big break and got the promotion she had been working on for 11 years. During the negotiation process, she asked for an extra 10% raise because she was moving from a state with no state tax to a state that paid state tax. Human Resources told her it shouldn't be a problem, that was normal for these situations and to talk to her boss and they would work it out. She never got the raise and was told she should be happy to have received the promotion.

KRT Recap

Neither Human Resources nor Janet's new boss did the right thing. If the KRT model was being used, this would have never happened. Human Resources would have handled the issue and it would have never fallen into Janet's lap to handle.

According to an interview with Sheryl Sandberg (COO of Facebook), the message was clear: Men need to care enough about gender equality to act.[82] There are four main things that we can do to help each other:

- Need to aggressively push against biases
- Give women the credit they deserve
- Don't make assumptions about what women want
- Make professional connections with women

Yes, both men and women are important for gender equality. We need to work together to make the change we want to see in the business world. We need to support each other and work toward a more diverse senior leadership team. 2017 was a record year for women CEOs. The Fortune 500 companies now have 27 female CEOS, which is up from 2016 of 21. Even with this little increase, that is still only 5.4% of the CEOS. And only three Fortune 500 companies have black male leaders. No companies are led by black women.

Almost half of all women who work in technology eventually leave the field. Not because they don't have the skills, because they are being paid less, they are harassed, and the company doesn't care about the fair and equitable treatment of their employees. This turnover "tech leavers" costs Silicon Valley more than $16 billion each year. Yet, they do nothing to resolve the problem. If they were losing 50% of their male employees, you know they would actually look into the issue and try to resolve it. So, it is up to

---

[82]Fessler, "Sandberg."

women and their allies to fight this battle to make a more equitable workplace.

Men want to sidestep the issue by never being alone with women and not be willing to mentor women. This will not get us to the future. This is the status quo. Men need to acknowledge their fear and that it is ok to ask questions. Change is not easy, but as par for the course, the only way out of this mess is through it. We must have the hard conversations.

It's time for women to own their power and start helping each other. We have been taught to justify our actions by explaining why we do what we do. It's time we stop justifying our actions and start being vocal about the problems. We must come to work each day knowing that we have the power to be the change we need.

> *"The companies who will own the future are the ones that are brave in this moment. The ones that retreat and take the safe route. They will be left behind."*
>
> **—Kat Gordon**
> Entrepreneur

KRT Recap

The Bad and Ugly that you just learned about is our reality. It is time we stand up and say, "No more!" We must demand better from our companies and from ourselves. We must speak out and take a stand for our future. It's no wonder that employees do not respect or trust their employers. They have seen all of this for decades and nothing has changed.

Leading our future with the KRT model will not only create an optimized workforce, but it will transform companies from the inside out. The new rules for Human Resources use the KRT model to specify the issues that must be addressed for our future. By treating employees first with kindness and then building to respect, imagine the transformation you will see. Your employees' psychological safety will increase with each step leading to happier and healthier employees, which, in turn, will help increase your company's profitability and productivity.

3

THIS ISN'T ROCKET SCIENCE

CUSTOMER EXPERIENCE

In the last two chapters, there was a great deal of information, including facts that some of us wish weren't true. To move into the future, we have to face all of the truths no matter how unscrupulous they may be. Some people only see the problems as something that can never be fixed because **it is what it is**. I am not that person. I am the optimistic person who knows that we can make the changes needed for the future. In this chapter, we are going to see how the data fits carefully into the KRT model as it relates to three main areas in any business: customer experience, employee engagement, and leadership.

During my career, I kept a collection of books that I would reference to help the managers I was mentoring. One of these books was *The Simple Truths of Service: Inspired by Johnny the Bagger.*[83] In this short book, Barbara Glanz gives an interesting take on customer service. Johnny was a bagger in a grocery store and didn't think he could do anything special for the customers. One day, Johnny decided to create a "thought for the day" and print out and give it to each customer. Within a month, there were lines of people waiting to checkout to get Johnny's thought of the day. These people did not want to be checked out faster, they wanted to wait to see Johnny. Johnny showed that the little things do matter, and that showing kindness can make an immense difference to any company. Do you want to be Johnny today?

What does Great Service do?

- Inspires stories
- Uses outside the box thinking
- Is a choice
- Starts with a clear vision
- Requires that everyone catch the vision
- Surprises people
- Begins with anyone
- Goes the extra mile
- Brings customers back
- The final truth – GREAT SERVICE COMES FROM THE HEART

Do you ever feel like businesses really don't want your money or business? Have you ever called about your bill and the person

---

[83]Blanchard and Glanz, *The Simple Truths of Service.*

on the other end didn't seem to care? Have you seen an employee being yelled at while working? Have you had your food shoved out the drive-through window at you without a word being spoken?

Customers want
great service
from happy
employees

Even kindergarten classes have rules that translate into the business world such as:

- Listen when others are talking
- Show respect for school and personal property
- Be kind to others

If our society is still being taught these good behaviors and teachers are holding their students accountable, why aren't businesses holding their managers/employees accountable? Why do they keep allowing the Adult Bullies to win?

Officially, your employer cannot force you to be happy at work. But wouldn't your job be so much better if you were happy at work and your employer was using the KRT model? Would you be more productive if you felt like you were valued? It's a real simple formula. Treating employees with kindness and respect will help increase sales, decrease turnover, and increase NPS on all sides. So, why don't businesses pay attention?

In 2018, we have seen more job vacancies nationwide than the number of unemployed people. Some would say this shows our economy is working well. But when you dig into what is happening, you will quickly see that workers are quitting their jobs at the highest rate in over a decade to get away from their toxic work environments. This has led to customer service deteriorating because companies are willing to hire someone who isn't qualified instead of raising the wages of someone who is. Companies care more about the bottom line than their employees and this can be seen in customer service everywhere.

Big Business is no longer run to provide jobs and good living to their employees. *They are being run for greed.* Greed has taken over as the number one goal. Wells Fargo CEO lined his pockets with money because of the illegal sales practices that his company was doing. EpiPen raised their price so much it made it unaffordable for the people who needed it most—just so the execs could make more money. These examples could not have occurred unless Human Resources and Legal agreed.

Company data for two companies who have been involved with scandals (Executive officers—C-suite per their company websites).

Company	Male	Female	Under 45-years-old
Wells Fargo	7	3	0
EpiPen (Mylan)	4	1	0

Data pulled 6.5.18

Just looking at these two examples, you will easily see that women and people under 45 are not represented proportionally. This is no surprise. Also, there is very little diversity and inclusion being seen in the C-suite of these companies.

Now let's look at two companies that have high customer satisfaction.

Company	Male Board Members	Female Board Members	Under 45-years-old
Facebook	4	1	2
Google	4	1	3

Recap:

- Women are still not at the C-suite in proper proportion.
- Executive teams who are younger are performing better for customer satisfaction.

An example of KRT in action is the Starbucks announcement on January 26, 2017 which shows that they plan to add three new diverse directors to their board. The new Starbucks board would be a total of 14 people with 36% minority and 29% women.[84] By changing the board, Starbucks will become more diverse and will be able to learn about different cultures to help make their product better across the board. This change made is easier for Starbucks to act fast when the bias incident occurred in 2018.

How does greed affect customer experience?

- Bad selling decisions such as setting up accounts or selling products the customer has stated they do not want to purchase.
- Placing customers on contracts to keep services and products with the customer. Contract language has been made to be confusing and allows the contract to be automatically renewed without customer permission.
- Employee dissatisfaction around corrupt sales practices.

---

[84]Feldberg and Kim, "Starbucks."

- Customers who spend more money are treated better (in companies that sell more than one service).
- Rewarding cheaters with incentives, which encourages more cheating.
- Sales reps selling items/solutions that are not available for sale and passing to operations to figure it out how to provide.

> *"In the old world, you devoted 30% of your time to building a great service and 70% of your time to shouting about it. In the new world, that inverts."*
>
> **—Jeff Bezos**
> CEO of Amazon

KRT Inaction—Rewarding cheaters example

Mina was a top performer for her team and was invited to the Top Sellers event in Orlando, Florida. This was a huge deal for Mina, and she was so proud. She brought her best friend Maria with her to the event. They got to go to Disney World, Epcot, and even got free massages.

During the recognition event, Mina was mingling with other sellers. She asked how many sales they had. Ned stated he had on average 120 sales per month. Mina was amazed because she was only averaging 100. She asked him how he did it. Ned states "I tell people there is a money-back guarantee and they will not be charged if they don't like the product." Mina finished the conversation and excused herself.

Mina became confused because she knows that the company doesn't have a money-back guarantee and that all customers will be charged. The only way a customer got a credit was to call into the call center and request one. When she returns to the office, Mina asks her manager Roger if there is a new "money-back program" that she didn't know about. Her manager tells her, "No." Mina then explains what she heard at the event. Her manager states he will investigate and get back with her.

The next day, Roger confirms that there is no such policy and if Ned was selling that way, he should stop immediately. Roger then calls Ned's manager to let him know what was being said. Ned's manager states that sales are competitive and what Ned is doing is approved by him. Roger cannot believe what he is hearing. Roger immediately calls Human Resources to report the issue.

Human Resources does nothing. Ned and Ned's manager still work for the business.

KRT Recap

Ned and Ned's manager were not doing the right thing and they knew what they were doing was wrong. If they were using the KRT model, this type of behavior would not have happened because the company would not be rewarding this type of cheating behavior.

What if companies had to report to their customers/ shareholders each month, quarter, year how many customers stated they did not order a product or service? The numbers would astonish anyone. One department I worked with had numbers in the 30% to 40% range. The bad sellers and their managers were rewarded with commission and incentives. The sellers' managers did nothing to stop the behavior. Corporate America has decided that excuses and lies are easier to deal with, such as, the customer changed their mind, they agreed at the time, and my favorite I talked with the husband and now the wife wants to cancel.

Greed is the guiding factor for a lot of businesses, but there is hope on the horizon. More small businesses are being created with employees, planet, community and integrity in mind. This is creating a shift in business. People are conscious of what they are consuming and are using their money to make their point. Consumers have choices and if we want change, then consumers need to use their resources and money to create that change.

1. If you want more products manufactured in the U.S., then stop buying products that are made outside the U.S.
2. If you were treated badly or had products placed on your account that you didn't order, then change companies.

We are at a decisive moment in history. Corporate America should be concerned. 87% of people believe business should place at least equal weight on business and society. *It's time for businesses to realize that the greed machine days are over and they cannot save it.* The old capitalist system is based on the scarcity mentality that there isn't enough and that you need to get as much as possible while giving up as little as possible. This model is changing, and it is time to pivot to a new way of doing business because the old way will no longer work.

Corporate social responsibility (CSR): Also called corporate conscience, corporate citizenship, or responsible business, it is a form of corporate self-regulation integrated into a business model. CSR policy functions as a self-regulatory mechanism whereby a business monitors and ensures its active compliance with the spirit of the law, ethical standards and national or international norms.

It's simple. Customers want/like ethical companies and are more likely to recommend them to their friends and family. CSR has been around since the 1960s, but the term is gaining more traction as our society evolves. Customers don't want to do business with cheaters, liars, and Adult Bullies.

Racism: Racial prejudice or discrimination

Prejudice: An irrational attitude of hostility directed against an individual, a group, a race, or their supposed characteristics

How does racism affect the customer experience (*New York Times* Hotel Experiment)?

- Employees are more likely to respond to emails when the name used is typically white.
- Employees provided 20% more restaurant recommendations to white people to other races.

- Employees were more polite to white people.
- 3× more likely to provide extra information (go above and beyond) to white people.

This experiment shows how employees at a hotel (we don't know their race) treat customers differently. This is a customer service nightmare. All customers are created equal and should not be treated differently. It is time for companies to follow in Starbucks' path and recognize their own racial bias. Companies can make the change if they are willing to step up and do the work.

Providing a good customer experience by using the KRT model for all customers is not rocket science. I will repeat…Providing good customer service is not rocket science. All of it starts at the top. There needs to be equitable diversity at the Executive and Board of Director levels. Once that happens, things will begin to change at all levels.

The bottom line is all the discrimination and harassment cost company's money. Plain and simple. Employees who have been treated badly will lower their productivity and maybe even leave. Don't forget the customers who your company treated badly because your employees weren't motivated to do a good job because of how they were treated. Treat your employees like crap and they, in turn, will treat your customers like crap. It's a vicious cycle that must stop.

THE REAL REASONS EMPLOYEES QUIT THEIR JOBS

Employees leave a company 80% of the time due to their manager. People are leaving people not companies. Employees are seeing the problems, Human Resources is not helping them, and they see no other way than to quit. Millennials are doing this, and people are quick to blame the generation. This is not a generation problem; this is a company culture problem. Companies are quick to blame the employee instead of looking internally at their own issues.

Top 9 reasons why people leave their jobs
- Belittling Culture/Lack of Leadership
  - Discrimination
  - Mentality of this is the way it has always been done and not learning from past mistakes
  - Not honoring commitments
  - Open cynicism
  - No fun
- Bad Bosses/Adult Bullies
  - Hostile work environment/yelling and screaming
  - Command and control mentality
  - Not trained how to handle problems and conflicts
  - Blame/shame game—bully tactic
  - Act like dictators
- No Coaching from Manager
  - Managers expect employees to be mindreaders
  - Cannot ask questions or perceived as stupid
  - Quick to criticize work
  - Focus on weaknesses and not strengths
- Bad Communication
  - No communication
  - Too many communications
  - Communications that top leaders send, but your leader tells you to ignore

- Favoritism
  - ○ Like high school cliques
  - ○ Promoting people not qualified for job (keeps Adult Bully in power)
- Lack of Praise and Recognition
  - ○ Scolding during team meetings
  - ○ Don't remember birthdays
- Micromanagement
- No Growth Potential
- Dumb Rules and Schedules
  - ○ No flexibility
  - ○ Too many meetings
  - ○ Too many documents saying the exact same thing

80% of employees leave because of their manager

The top reason is lack of leadership. Managers are getting promoted but not being given the skills they need to be successful. Just because a person is a top salesperson does not mean they can be a leader in the management world. Businesses have lots of managers, but very few leaders. Leadership cannot be obtained by getting the right title.

What does a bad boss/Adult Bully do to your health? Think about it. If you are yelled at on a consistent basis at work, you end up taking this hostile work environment into your private life. This type of constant hostile environment can lead to anxiety and depression. It is no coincidence that prescriptions for medications to help anxiety and depression are at an all-time high.

The 2018 CDC data is showing that suicide rates have increased in the U.S. from 1999 to the present by nearly 30%.[85] There are even states that have increased by up to 58%. Shouldn't this be concerning to everyone? We know how bullying in schools has led to school shootings. Why aren't we paying attention to what these Adult Bullies and companies are doing to us and our fellow Americans? Something is wrong with our culture and we must fix it. We have been valuing the wrong things. Nothing we can buy, own, or attain will make us feel whole in the long term.

> *"Getting to the place where you have everything everybody has ever desired and realizing you are still unhappy."*
>
> **—Jim Carrey**
> Actor

Employees are ready for a change. They no longer want to put up with these bad company cultures and Adult Bullies. They want the world to see that this type of behavior is not productive and we need to evolve into a better business model. Employees deserve kindness, respect, and trust.

Per the 2015 Gallup Survey, 41% of American workers say they have been "psychologically harassed" at their job.[86] Adult Bullies engage in behaviors that are destructive and enjoy being

---

[85]Powers, "Suicidal."
[86]Gregoire, "Toxic."

abusive to others. These Adult Bullies can be narcissistic and could have psychopath tendencies. The evidence is clear that the leadership qualities of Adult Bully bosses over time exerts a heavy toll on employees' health. The stress your boss causes is bad for your health and increases your chance of having a heart attack by as much as 50%.

REAL EMPLOYEE ENGAGEMENT

When a company has high employee turnover and bad customer service you can bet it is the company's culture. In today's world, the company's culture decides all outcomes. As we have discussed, the command and control style of culture and leadership is no longer going to work in the future. Companies who don't want to change their company culture will be left behind.

> **Company Culture:** The personality of a company. It defines the environment in which employees work. Company culture includes a variety of elements, including work environment, company mission, value, ethics, expectations, and goals.

Why is a company's culture so important? Let's look at the data. Less than one-third of all employees are satisfied with their job and 80% report that they are not engaged at work. To gain real employee engagement, companies need to change how they view their employees.

Employee Net Promoter Scores (eNPS) or any company survey like it is not working. When doing these surveys quarterly or yearly, the managers are not really looking at the results. They think when someone complains they are an outlier and they don't need to concern themselves with that complaint. They develop plans that never go anywhere, and nothing ever changes.

How do I know? I lived it repeatedly. I was always that outlier telling the truth. I remember sitting in the meetings with senior VPs and presidents and talking through the plans to help our employees. Not one of those plans ever took into consideration the outliers.

KRT Inaction—Company Culture example

Yasmin was a top director in her division. She was in the innovation side of the company and was creating new products and services. She had worked in many jobs on her way up to Director. In this new organization, within six months upper management decided to send out a survey to their employees. This survey was the same one they have been sending for years. The company wants to know what they are doing right and wrong from their employees anonymously.

Yasmin's team came up to her and told her that they didn't think the surveys were really anonymous and they were afraid to give their real thoughts. Yasmin explained that, yes, it was anonymous, but if you make a comment that is very specific, then, yes, they will figure out who you are. She told her team to be honest because, yes, there are major problems.

Yasmin wasn't afraid to walk the talk and she reported many items in the survey. Around one to two months later when the results came out, Yasmin was looking through them and noticed that many of the people who also had reported the same issues to her did not report them on the survey.

When upper leadership got together to discuss the plan to make changes going forward, the first thing Yasmin heard was: don't pay attention to the haters because they are just disgruntled employees. The Senior Vice President went on to discuss the results all the while praising the team for getting more than 50% of their employees to take the survey.

Yasmin was not surprised at all by the behavior because she had seen this same thing the past five years in other jobs. She always reported the issues and they always ignored them and categorized them as outliers.

KRT Recap

Upper management wanted to keep their blinders on. They did not want to listen to what their employees were telling them. If the KRT model was being used, then each item would be discussed and welcomed. The employees would have felt that their workplace was a safe place to talk about their issues and they would have filled out the survey truthfully. Then management would have acted accordingly to work through any problems.

What mattered to this company was not the results, but the percentage of employees who took the survey. They were going through the motions and trying to meet a metric instead of taking the time to look internally at their issues. Leaders pay attention to what they are measured on. If they are measured on what percentage of employees take a survey, then that is what they will achieve. Why do you think Wells Fargo had so many cheaters? They focused on the one metric.

Imagine what would happen if all employees told the truth. Employees are afraid their responses will be linked back to them and they will lose their jobs, or they see the hostile work environment with discrimination and believe that it is normal. This has been allowed to be commonplace for so long that we have forgotten the simple fact that leaders should care about the truth and work to fix their cultures.

Being yelled at by your boss while working is *not normal*.

Employee Engagement is a direct reflection of an organization's culture. I have seen companies that state they want their culture to be one way, but then they do the exact opposite. Employees have figured this out and have decided to report these issues in apps like Glassdoor. Glassdoor makes it easy for potential employees to look at how other employees' rate that company.

Fortune top 10 companies for 2018—2016 versus 2018 Glassdoor data (Glassdoor.com)

Name	2016		2018	
	# of Stars	Recommend to a friend	# of Stars	Recommend to a friend
Walmart	3.2	55%	3.2	55%
Exxon Mobil	3.8	75%	3.8	73%
Apple	4.0	80%	4.0	79%
Berkshire Hathaway	3.3	51%	2.8	45%

(Continued)

Name	2016		2018	
	# of Stars	Recommend to a friend	# of Stars	Recommend to a friend
McKesson	3.4	61%	3.3	60%
United HealthCare	3.8	80%	3.7	72%
CVS Health	2.7	36%	2.8	37%
General Motors	3.6	71%	3.7	72%
Amazon	n/a	n/a	3.8	74%
AT&T	3.4	62%	3.4	60%

Clearly, from the data you can see that there is plenty of room to grow. In fact, most companies got worse when comparing the data from just two years ago. Companies need to start looking at these scores and reviews to figure out what employees think. Companies should look at all the three-star (or fewer) reviews. Since this is anonymous, people tend to be more truthful. The truth may hurt, but if one person is reporting the issue *then there is most likely a bigger issue*. Employee Engagement is a fine line and if one manager is not on board, then the culture is broken. Per Deloitte, 83% of millennials are more engaged at work when it is in an inclusion environment.

"Always treat your employees exactly as you want them to treat your best customers."

—Stephen R. Covey
Influential Leadership Expert and Author

Keeping employees engaged is not just a one-and-done scenario. Using the KRT model for employee engagement must be worked on every single day. When a leader works on engaging their employees each day, they will build a cohesive team that will perform at their best. Isn't that what all companies should be striving for? The little things add up. We just need to be consistent and purposeful. It may be hard to measure in the short term, but the results in the long term are a game changer. The Google X team is a great example because they are encouraged to fail and learn from their failure. Imagine the psychological safety this team must feel.

The Kindness, Respect, and Trust (KRT) model is critical to helping all organizations perform at their best. To engage employees, this model gives you specific information for each step of the process. Everything starts with Kindness, moves to Respect, and eventually to Trust. The model is simple and straight the point. Here's the top 20 ways to engage your employees shown in the KRT model.

20 Ways to Engage Employees

Kindness:
- Stop yelling and screaming
- Stop allowing Adult Bullies
- Listen more
- Connection/inclusion
- Managers need to make employee success their goal
- Encourage—not command
- Be open-minded and allow for new ideas

Respect:
- Stop allowing discrimination
- Communicate the truth
- Stop playing favorites—avoid favoritism
- Praise in public and scold in private
- Managers need to admit when they are wrong
- Give credit when due (personalized)
- Be clear on what type of perfomance your company rewards

Trust:
- Flexibility (not just 9-to-5/maybe four-day weeks) and time off for volunteering
- Transparency
- Advancement and learning opportunities
- Follow through from management
- Collaboration
- Challenge

I bet I know what you are thinking. These 20 ways to engage your employees would create more productivity, increased sales, and happier employees. You would be right. So why don't all businesses do these things for their employees? That is a complex question. One answer is that we have normalized the bad behaviors we see in business and believe that is the way work must be. Large companies have allowed the greed and bad management to take precedence over their employees.

Employee Engagement exercises available at

www.bekindtoall.com

KRT Inaction—Employee Engagement: A New Hire Manager Story

Jolie joined the marketing department right out of college. She was so excited to have landed a job with a Fortune 100 company. She was happy with her salary and the town that she moved to. About two months into the job, Jolie started to see the favoritism her manager gave other employees. She worked 40–50 hours a week to make sure to give her manager everything that was needed even though her manager was too busy to answer questions.

Jolie was given a huge presentation to work on around Customer Buying Patterns. She worked very hard on the presentation. During the team meeting, she presented the data. Her boss didn't even pay attention during the presentation; she was too busy with her email. When she completed the presentation, her boss looked up and said, "That isn't what I asked you to do, go and redo it."

Jolie was heartbroken and very confused because she went back to the email sent by her boss and everything she asked for was in the presentation. Jolie goes to her manager and asks what she needs to change. Her boss tells her that the presentation needs to have a certain order. Jolie asks what the order is, and her manager tells her to go talk to a coworker and figure out on her own. Jolie does what is needed based on her coworker's recommendation and presents the data at the next meeting. Her manager states again during the meeting that the presentation is not right and she needs to get this right if she wants to keep her job. Jolie goes back to her manager for help and she takes away the project and gives to the coworker. The coworker changes only a few slides but basically leaves all the information intact. The coworker presents the data and the manager praises the coworker. At this point, Jolie is defeated. What did she do wrong? During her evaluation, her manager lists out that she does not know how to follow directions and is not a team player. Jolie tries to talk with her manager about what can be done to make things better. The manager tells her to do a better job and be more like her coworker. Jolie leaves the department and they do not do an exit interview.

KRT Recap

Jolie's boss was not making her employee's success her goal. She was more worried about not helping Jolie. If the KRT model was being used, Jolie's boss would have helped her with the presentation and spent the time to get to know her.

Is it any wonder employees aren't engaged at work? Jolie was not given a chance to succeed because her manager did not care about her success. This is where you start to see the clear line between being a manager and being a leader. When respect is absent, that is when morale problems occur and productivity declines. Jolie is now a director at another company and is a leader in her business.

KRT Inaction—Respect and Truth example

Viola has worked for Amand for approximately one year. Amand wants to make decisions on everything without adequate information. Amand likes to blame people and yell and scream when things do not go "flawlessly." Amand does not trust or respect his employees.

Viola is tired of her manager making decisions and not understanding the outcomes. His latest decision made the sales systems stop working. During their weekly meeting, Viola explained to him what happened and how Viola's team fixed the sales systems. She explained how trust and respect was key to any relationship. Amand took offense to the discussion and told Viola that trust and respect has nothing to do with business. She needed to go do her job and stop making waves.

KRT Recap

Amand is clearly not working with his employees' interests on the forefront. He is still working in the command and control culture. If the KRT model was being used, then Viola's concerns would have been listened to and discussed. Amand would not be yelling, screaming, and blaming people. He would be using problem-solving and conflict-resolution skills to find the best solution.

Is it any wonder that employees don't talk to their managers when there are issues? Many managers do not trust or respect their employees. If businesses want to succeed in the future, these types of behaviors must stop. Engagement of employees is the key to success. Without the proper psychological safety at their job, employees will allow a culture of silence instead of listening.

WHAT IS A KRT LEADER?

There is a clear difference between being a leader and being a manager. Businesses have not been teaching their managers how to be leaders. Instead, companies are allowing and praising the bad behaviors and the Human Resources department does nothing to stop these bad behaviors and hostile work environments. In a lot of cases, Human Resources just lends a blind eye, especially if the person is an upper manager. This is the type of behavior that will hurt any project and company. It is time that the destructive behavior is ended.

Leadership is learned and not given by your title

Remember the number one reason why employees don't like their jobs or are disengaged on the job has to do with their boss. There are so many articles on the internet about how to deal with your bad boss or how to quit when your boss is nightmare. It doesn't help any of us when these articles don't state to report these Adult Bullies to Human Resources. In fact, one article from Thrive Global states the following: "To anyone reading this right now who may be facing a similar situation, don't let your nightmare boss be the cause of you leaving your job. If you can't take it anymore, then leave, but no one has the right to be treated badly by a senior executive. If you want to show them up, then work hard and earn the rewards you deserve—don't let them win."[87] Just reading these words should make your cringe. Basically, suck it up buttercup and let the bad boss keep their job all the while you keep your mouth shut and try to prove your worth. This is not what we should be teaching anyone.

What makes a great KRT leader? Caring about your employees. Employees don't care what their managers want them to do until they know how much their manager cares about them. Employees need to know that their manager cares or whatever words they use don't matter.

Leadership is a skill that you develop and work on daily. Just because you got the title does not make you a leader. It takes practice and hard work. You will make mistakes, but if you are honest and willing to learn, you will become better each day. I know I have not always been the best the leader, which is hard for some people to admit to themselves. I have made mistakes and I have failed, but I always owned my mistakes and I learned from my failures. It's how you handle these situations/failures that shows your true leadership skills. Here are the top 20 characteristics of a leader shown in the KRT model.

---

[87]Ghosh, "Nightmare."

Top 20 Characteristics of a KRT Leader

Kindness:
- Humility and empathy
- Able to listen before speaking
- Can build a relationship with employees
- Authentic and genuine
- Knows how to handle problems and conflicts without yelling
- Welcomes diversity, difference of options, and lives outside of work
- Curious and optimistic—Can ask, "What if...?"
- Has fun, is creative, celebrates successes

Respect:
- Honest/truthful
- Has their teams' back, cares about their employee careers
- Coaches and teaches, does not dictate
- Shows respect toward all employees—does not scold in public
- Is responsible—follows through/explains the "why"
- Keeps promises (integrity)
- Motivates and inspires others/builds ownership
- Confident
- Does not play the blame game/shares credit

Trust:
- Wants change
- Sticks to Convictions/Make them proud
- Delegates

This list correlates with the employee engagement information. Employees want to be treated with kindness, respect, and trust. They don't want to work for a company that discriminates and allows managers to act like Adult Bullies. The Adult Bully is not a leader. Employees are tired of the Adult Bullies winning and not being held responsible for their actions. It is time for all companies to look at their managers and decide if they are a leader or an Adult Bully. With shifting core values of what a job is, this is imperative for employee engagement and retention.

According to *Good to Great* by Jim Collins, "We found no systematic pattern linking executive compensation to the process of going from good to great."[88] This means that money doesn't matter

---

[88]Collins, *Good to Great*.

when it comes to creating a leader. Being a leader isn't about the money, it is about creating an environment for people to thrive.

Even at Davos—World Economic Forum, it can be seen that that our world is changing. 75% of CEOS agree that it is important to have a strong corporate purpose reflected in values, culture, and behaviors. They know diversity and better leadership must be embraced within their organizations. Yet, they still have not made the historical shift in what they are doing.

A great KRT leader recognizes everyone's contribution. They understand that all assignments are not created equal. For example, office housework/cleanup such as helping with a lunch meeting and getting the coffee are different from other assignments. This type of work needs to be equally divided between all team members and not just given to women. They also know that the "high-profile/get noticed" projects also need to be assigned out equally.

KRT in Action—Leader example

Tammy is a Vice President with a territory of the East Coast. Tammy has over 2,000 employees who work in her organization. Tammy has a staff of four employees who handle all day-to-day projects and employee needs. Tammy has spent many hours with each of her staff to learn more about them. Tammy knows her employees and which one is best equipped to handle which project.

Tammy goes into her region on a regular basis to work with her sales employees and the union to get better sales results. Tammy is always open, honest, and has her employees' backs. She does not discriminate and always wants to listen to different points of view. Tammy is always calm and collected and never yells. The union states, "Tammy is one of the most compassionate leaders they have worked with. She really listens to our concerns."

KRT Recap

Tammy knows that leading with kindness, showing empathy, welcoming diversity, and communicating the truth will lead to productive teams that perform at peak states.

A KRT leader spends time with their team. They allow their employees to make mistakes. They know employees need flexibility. They do not define themselves by their job. They define themselves by how they treat people. They walk the walk and talk the talk. They have work life balance and want the same for their employees.

"Leadership is based on inspiration, not domination; on cooperation, not intimidation."

—William Arthur Ward
Writer

KRT Recap

This section just revealed the roadmap of specific actions that are needed for our future. These actions are as easy as being honest, admitting when you make a mistake, and having fun. All of the research about customers, employees, and leaders fall easily into the different segments of the KRT model. Leading with kindness leads to respect, which will then lead to trust. You must build from the bottom to the top.

To be a KRT leader for the future, you must be purposeful with your actions. You must pay attention and actually listen. You will have to do uncomfortable things that will stretch you in ways you never knew. The time for being quiet is over. The time for action and change is upon us. Are you ready?

PART II

4

KINDNESS, RESPECT, AND TRUST (KRT) MODEL

In this chapter, we are going to learn the three steps of the KRT model. Since these terms are simple and we have learned them most of our lives, we are going to look at specific examples. By looking at these examples, you will be able to gain more insight and practical knowledge for implementing the changes needed.

Implementing the KRT model is not just about following the steps. It's about making changes on how you interact with your team. Changing yourself to notice when you aren't being your best self. Noticing the microaggressions, reporting the bad behaviors/ Adult Bullies. Not allowing Human Resources to gaslight you. Paying attention to details that you may have not noticed before. Change is never instantaneous; it will take time and you will make mistakes. The important part is that you are honest and are willing to be a role model.

While moving into the future, we need to keep three very important resources in mind.

- People
- Planet
- Animals

These three resources encompass everything that is valuable in the society we live in. We need to treat these things as finite resources and make sure we are caring for these resources. When we mistreat one of these resources, there are repercussions to all. Due to greed and bad practices, businesses have lost touch on what matters. It's time for us to go back to the basics.

The KRT model is simple and straight to the point:

- Kindness leads to Respect
- Respect leads to Trust
- You cannot have Trust without both Kindness and Respect

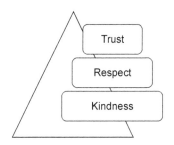

Definitions

Kindness: (noun) the quality of being friendly, generous, and considerate

Respect: (noun) a feeling of deep admiration for someone or something elicited by their abilities, qualities, or achievements

Trust: (noun) firm belief in the reliability, truth, ability, or strength of someone or something

Connection and authenticity are keys to implementing the KRT model. We have talked about empathy and gratitude, which will be key strengths that you will need to develop. By learning the KRT model, you will be able to improve yourself, your team, and your company. The skills you will learn will also play into your social and family life.

This model works by implementing kindness on a consistent basis. When you do this, you will see other parts of your life change. Your attitude toward failure will become one of failing forward and learning instead of blame and shame. Your psychological wellbeing will also improve because mentally we feel good when we are kind to other people.

I truly believe we are all compassionate people who want to do the right thing. We have just lost our way. In homage to the KISS method, which if you don't know, is Keep it Simple Stupid, I have created the KRT model. Connection is the #1 form of currency right now. Those who learn how to connect and do the right thing will be the leaders that tomorrow needs. Are you ready to learn how?

STEP 1—KINDNESS

- *Kindness* is the foundation to create and build relationships.
- *Kindness* can be absent in business. Whether it is how the business treats their employees or how they treat their customers.

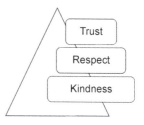

Where did the kindness go? I have been asking myself this question for years. I watched business change and become greedier and less compassionate about their employees. I worked each day to keep my integrity and bring kindness to all situations. This wasn't easy, but I kept my head high and I marched on, which is what most of us are doing right now.

I remember growing up, I thought it was strange to have someone hold a door open for me. I was quite capable of doing that myself. What I didn't realize is that this is a gesture of kindness toward another person. Seriously, how hard is to hold open a door for someone? So, this simple gesture led to a societal experiment that I conducted in 2015.

In Atlanta, Georgia, I was walking into work and noticed that the man in front of me didn't even bother to hold the door open for me. This was a building that was dedicated to the business I worked for. So, the next day I went in and out of the building 20 times to see what would happen. I followed ten men and ten women into the building. Four out of ten men held the door open for me. Six out of the ten women held the door open for me. So only 50% of the time were people kind enough to worry about the person behind them entering the building. Then I conducted the experiment at a mall in Texas. The results were shockingly similar. Four out of ten men held the door open and eight out of ten women held the door open. So, the results were 60%, but women were much more likely to hold the door open.

Based on this data, I decided to change the experiment to focus on me holding the door open for others. At my workplace, I did this 20 times in two days to see if people would say thank you to me for holding the door open. The results weren't much different, five out of ten men said thank you and six out of ten women said thank you, for a total of 55% thanking me. When I recreated this experiment at the mall in Texas, I was pleasantly surprised with increased thank yous. Seven out of ten men and eight out of ten women thanked me, for a total of 70%.

These quick experiments show that at a workplace, employees are around 50% kind, while out in public people show more kindness around 65% of the time. If a person is not treated with kindness at their job, why would they treat others with kindness? Why don't you try this experiment at your job and see what happens?

I was taught that being nice to people was a great trait but being too nice would lead to trouble. People would want to take advantage of my kindness. Well, yes, some people have taken advantage, I will not deny that fact. Even though this has happened, I will not stop being a kind and giving person. I know people who have been hurt so many times because for their kindness, they believe everyone is out to get them. This is simply not the case. We need more kindness in the world. We need for people to smile at other people. We need compliments and gratitude.

Gratitude: The quality of being thankful; readiness to show appreciation for and to return kindness

---

Imagine having gratitude as part of your daily life. What if you could wake up each morning and say what you are grateful for instead of pushing the snooze button and delaying your life? Gratitude is a key component to living life to the fullest. If you are always upset over the little things like your Amazon box not arriving, you don't have time to worry about the bigger items. Seriously...how many times have your friends posted how pissed they are, or it is the end of the world that they didn't get their package? If something is that important, we need to get off our butt and go out and buy in a store. It's time we stop being the apathetic instant gratification nation. It's time we open our eyes to what we can become instead of what we are right now.

Why are we worried more about what makeup a celebrity is wearing instead of the homeless children in our community? Why do trust the words of known liars and frauds over people with education and knowledge? Why do we feel that we are unworthy if we are not rich? Why do we base everything in our lives on what we have versus who we are? These are hard questions to answer if you haven't thought about this before.

Do you want to do the self-discovery to learn more about what your true values really are?

Go to www.bekindtoall.com

Our society is realizing that money is not the key to happiness. Just look at the magazine rack while at the store. Most likely you will see an article about the keys to happiness. Compassion for your fellow man and kindness are the real keys. I want to personally thank the millennial generation for helping open our eyes.

Kindness is free, yet alludes a lot of us. Kindness is a mindset that creates good feelings and positive results. Let's all press reset and start living in a world where we value all human beings. We must stop being so self-absorbed and start giving back and caring about others.

Here are a few ways you can demonstrate kindness in business and the rest of your life:

- Be nice to all employees (even if they are not).
- Show respect to all employees.
- Be polite.
- Help someone in need.
- Help others succeed.

STEP 2—RESPECT

- *Respect* cannot be achieved without taking the time to learn about the person and kindness is the key to learning.
- *Respect* is absent in business, whether it is how the business treats their customers or how their treat their employees.

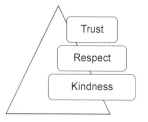

Respect is earned. Somewhere along the line, business decided that respect for money was more important than respect for their employees. We have been taught to respect the mighty dollar bill and how we get more of them. The lack of respect for anyone but yourself is how Adult Bullies keep continuing their work. They treat employees like garbage, Human Resources allows them to do this, and then people believe they don't deserve to be respected and that it is ok to be treated this way.

A few months before I quit my last job, I had had enough of the toxic work environment. Human Resources was ignoring my complaint (they did this for almost five months with no response). I went into my manager's office to discuss the issues yet again. Numerous team members were seeing the issues and they were all coming to me for help. Why me? Because I respected them and they respected me to do the right thing, even if I wasn't their manager. After being told again that I was wrong about the situation, I stated, "Don't we do all of this for the respect and trust of our employees?" My manager had no idea what to say. It was like these words were foreign. My manager did her job for greed and recognition. She never did her job for her team. She was never a servant leader.

STEP 3 – TRUST

- In any productive relationship, ***trust*** is the final layer that is built.
- After being kind to someone and building respect toward each other, ***trust*** is the overwhelming final piece that does take time.

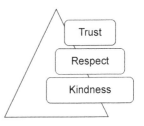

A mighty strong word—TRUST. Trust is critical for any business and without trust that business can/will fail. That is why there are so many books and trainings around trust. You may have heard of the following books: *The Speed of Trust* and *Smart Trust* by Stephen Covey. These are great foundations and great reads. I have taught *The Speed of Trust* in my mentoring circles for years. I am not here to rehash what those books teach us, instead we need to explore what trust means today.

Managers need their employees to trust them and managers need to trust their employees. This fact will never change. Without trust, the business cannot run effectively or efficiently. Imagine how much you and your organization can accomplish once you get to this top level.

KRT MODEL EXAMPLES

KRT works because it encompasses the whole person/organization and not just piece parts. By starting with kindness, you will get to know your employees. This is such an easy thing to do, yet many managers I have interviewed don't know where to start. So, let's learn from examples.

Kindness

KRT Inaction—No kindness example

Alayna was a brand-new employee at large retail store. She was excited for her job and how it will help pay for college. Alayna's manager is David. David has been with the business for 15 years and is a self-proclaimed team player. Alayna is now one of eight people on David's team. At their first team meeting, David introduced the team to Alayna. Then David went straight into work and deadlines. After the meeting, two coworkers offer to help Alayna with anything she needs. She is so grateful to see some friendly faces. After Alayna completed one month on the job, she has a review with David. During the review, David does not get to know Alayna, he just reads from his paper about her performance and lets her go back to work. As you can see, David is not showing any interest in getting to know his employee. How do you think Alayna feels about this?

Alayna works for the company for another two months and decides to quit. During the Human Resources exit interview, Alayna tells them that her manager didn't get to know her. He didn't care about the team, all he cared about was making sales goals. He couldn't spell or say her name correctly, even though she corrected him numerous times. She told Human Resources, how she is not the only one that feels this way.

KRT In Action—Kindness example

Terrell was a brand-new call center agent. He was excited to be part of a new team. Terrell's manager Tess was also excited he was on the team. At their first team meeting, Tess played some ice breaker games with her team so they could get to know each other better. After the meeting, Tess and Terrell were discussing his new job. Tess wanted to make sure that Terrell knew she was there to help him. She had been in his shoes once and knows how hard it could be. She was a single mother at the time and the schedule was hard, but she made it work. Terrell told Tess that he was still in college and was getting his BA in marketing. The exchange continued for almost 30 minutes. After the meeting, Terrell felt like a team member.

Easy ways to display kindness:

- Sharing information about yourself to create an environment of truth and sharing with your employees.
- Knowing your employee's birthdays, anniversary dates, children's names, pets, personal information they are willing to share.
- Using the above information to learn about each other. Without knowing this information about each other, you cannot respect each other

How To Engage Your Employees:

Kindness:
- Stop yelling and screaming
- Stop allowing Adult Bullies
- Listen more
- Connection/inclusion
- Managers need to make employee success their goal
- Encourage—not command
- Be open-minded and allow for new ideas

Some of you may be saying, "Of course I do all the things listed above." Congratulations! You are leading with kindness. It's now time for you to branch out to help others do the same. Kindness will always make a relationship stronger. Once it is strong enough, you will respect each other.

Respect

KRT Inaction—No respect example

Mike worked for a fast food restaurant for the past three years. His manager Lucy is a micromanager and must control everything the team does. One day Mike comes to work and looks very upset. Lucy doesn't say a thing to him. About halfway through his shift, Mike goes to talk to Lucy. Mike's dog had died the night before and he was wondering if he could take some time off today to handle the remains. Lucy denied the request and states, "Since you are already here—you should just stay, it's really not a big deal." Mike works the rest of his shift. The next day he puts in his two weeks' notice. Mike does not want to work for anyone who doesn't respect him as a person. He wasn't leaving the company—just the manager.

KRT In Action—Respect example

Anna is a salesperson for a time share vacation organization. She has worked for the organization for over two years. Her manager Cary is very kind and generous with the team. One day an emergency happened with Anna's brother. She went straight to Cary and let him know what was going on. Cary told Anna that her family was very important to take what time she needed to help her family. He told her they would work out her hours/vacation time when she got back. Anna left knowing that Cary respects her and he didn't question the situation more than what she wanted to speak to.

Easy ways to give respect:

- Respect is given and gained by being truthful with your employees. If your employee believes you are being untruthful, you will never get their respect.
- Telling the truth is a critical for building respect for each other.
- Once mutual kindness and respect have occurred you can move to trust

How To Engage Your Employees:

Respect:
- Stop allowing discrimination
- Communicate the truth
- Stop playing favorites—avoid favoritism
- Praise in public and scold in private
- Managers need to admit when they are wrong
- Give credit when due (personalized)
- Be clear on what type of perfomance your company rewards

Trust

KRT Inaction—No Trust example

Felicia has worked for a coffee shop for the past nine months. Her manager Rachael doesn't know anything about her. Felicia has tried to be kind to Rachael, but Rachael feels that work is for work. One night, Felicia was the last person working (one person called out ill).

When it was time, Felicia closed the store and started all the paperwork and cleanup. Rachael comes out of her office and starts yelling at Felicia because she was doing things in the wrong order. Yet, Felicia was doing exactly as her coworkers have taught her. Rachael takes over and starts barking orders at Felicia. As they finish closing, Rachael states that she was thinking of Felicia for a promotion but now she isn't so sure.

Because Felicia and Rachael never had kindness, they never could respect each other. Therefore, no trust was available.

KRT In Action—Trust example

Bart is an IT specialist for a Fortune 100 company. His manager Ollie has more than 20 years of experience in IT. Ollie has always believed that each person is a great resource and has treated his employees with kindness and respect. Ollie's wife decided to surprise him with a cruise for his birthday. About a week before the cruise, an emergency IT release was scheduled for Ollie's birthday.

Instead of worrying about how he was going to tell his wife he couldn't go, Ollie knew that Bart would be able to handle the IT release without any help from him. Ollie talked with Bart about the release and created a game plan before he goes on vacation. Bart handled the IT release with minimal issues, and the issues that did occur could be fixed within two days. When Ollie got back from his cruise, Bart briefed him on the release. Ollie thanked Bart with kindness and respect for the great work.

Easy ways to show Trust:

- Creating an environment of kindness and respect will lead to trust naturally. Once trust has been obtained, it is very important that this trust is not broken, or you will need to start from the beginning.
- Trust your team to meet their deadlines and don't hover over them to get them completed.
- Coach your team when there are new things for them to learn.

How To Engage Your Employees:

Trust:
- Flexibility (not just 9-to-5/maybe four-day weeks) and time off for volunteering
- Transparency
- Advancement and learning opportunities
- Follow-through from management
- Collaboration
- Challenge

5

MUST-HAVE LEADERSHIP SKILLS

C ommunication is the transmissions of one's thoughts or knowledge to another in a way that is clearly understood. In today's business world, communication is a key critical success factor in accomplishing everything from daily tasks to large projects. With the advent of all the new technologies, interpersonal communication skills are more vital than ever. Coupled with both employees and managers' time constraints, the skills you will learn are important and useful in both the business environment and in daily life.

Critical KRT Skills needed:
1. Active Listening
2. Problem-Solving
3. Conflict Resolution
4. Giving and Receiving Feedback

These skills take time and practice to master. These critical skills are not taught in most manager training. Usually what is learned are the specifics of the job, not how to handle your team. You can always practice these skills with your colleagues and mentors. The practice will help both of you.

Always
Remember
Kindness

Using the KRT model and these skills is what will set anyone apart as being an excellent leader. Have you ever been in a meeting (or conference call) where everyone is screaming over everyone else and nothing is getting done? That is because you have a room full of employees (including Adult Bullies) who have no idea how to handle the situation. They learned from their past managers and they truly believe that they know the right way. **This is a total waste of time and he/she who yells the loudest gets their way.** This way of handling business is not efficient and usually ends up as a costly experience for the business. This way of handling business will become obsolete as the command and control cultures are dying.

Now, let's look into details of four critical KRT leadership skills. At the end of each section is an example of the critical skill and how to perform it in a positive way.

Tips and Tricks:

- Rapport is key. Comfortable environment with no victim-blaming.
- Be an active participant.
- Don't allow distractions.
- Compromise.
- Pay attention to the language you use (always stay positive).

Want more practice?

Go to
www.bekindtoall.com/skills

ACTIVE LISTENING

Active Listening involves not only hearing what the speaker is saying, but truly understanding. The skill of Active Listening enables the listener to become a sounding board for the speaker. Active Listening also involves empathy on behalf of the listener, which will promote a better understanding of the speaker's situation or problem.

The purpose of Active Listening is not to solve the speaker's problem, but rather to understand the speaker's situation or problem and help facilitate a solution generated by the speaker.

There are seven steps to KRT Active Listening:

1. Find a quiet room and do not allow interruptions
2. Allow the other person (speaker) to control the conversation and solve his/her own problem
   a. Do not judge the person for anything
   b. Let them speak their mind
3. Ask open-ended questions
   a. Probe for clarification
   b. Use sparingly direct closed-ended questions

4. Reflect the speaker's emotions and nonverbal cues
   a. Take notes and pay attention
   b. Match the emotional tone
5. Probe for clarification
   a. Ask clarifying questions
6. Summarize what has been discussed for understanding
7. End session with kindness
   a. Convey the other person is important
   b. End with a handshake/fist bump etc.

For Active Listening to work, the listener must be just that, a LISTENER. The listener must stay away from leading questions and giving advice. This step is the hardest for most people. We want to help solve all the problems and help all the people. But being a leader means that you let your own team work on their issues and you are there to listen (NOT JUDGE) the person. When performed correctly, the conversation will encourage empathy and understanding for both parties.

Active Listening Example:

You are an employee at a new startup marketing business. You just graduated college and love your job. You have a lot of ideas and are eager to share them.

Aaron is your coworker and has been on the job for almost three months. He has been with the business the longest. He feels since he was there from the beginning, that he knows more than his coworkers.

Aaron has an issue he would like to discuss with you around the system problems he has been seeing.

Now practice the scenario using the above instructions.

PROBLEM-SOLVING

Problem-solving helps develop many solutions to a problem and allows all parties involved to choose a solution that is acceptable to all. Problem-solving does not allow who yells the loudest to get their way or allow the blame game to be played. Problem-solving is about logical discussion on what is truly going on, not what people perceive is happening.

There are six steps to KRT Problem-Solving:

1. Find a quiet room and do not allow interruptions. Include all applicable parties who need to be there and participate in finding a win/win solution.
   a. Describe the end goal
   b. There is no loser
   c. No yelling
2. Describe the problem in detail (one slide max in Power Point)
3. Ask for team members' input and information related to the problem
   a. Allow all parties to speak and not interrupt each other
   b. Actively Listen (use steps)
      • Provide supportive verbal and nonverbal behavior
   c. Document discussion on whiteboard/computer/paper
   d. Encourage variety of solutions (not what we have always done/outside the box/brainstorm)
4. Summarize all constraints, issues, and needs
5. Choose and agree on acceptable solution for all parties involved.
   a. This is not a dictatorship—all parties are equally important

6. End session with kindness
   a. Convey all parties involved are important
   b. End with a handshake/fist bump etc.

During this process, all people involved need to be made to feel welcome. The speaker needs to make sure not to make the other person or team member defensive. If the other person is made to feel defensive, then the situation may escalate to a situation that could have been avoided (such as yelling). It is important that both sides come up with as many solutions as possible and that all sides participate in generating solutions. All sides contribute to the final solution.

Problem-Solving Example:

You are a manager of a retail store. The store is open from 10 a.m. to 9 p.m. Monday through Saturday and 12 to 6 p.m. on Sundays, except for holidays. Your team consists of four assistant managers. These managers have specific departments and responsibilities.

The retail store has been struggling with sales. The number of customers who are visiting the store has declined by 25% but their sales have gone down by 30%.

Allison is the Human Resources manager and does all of the hiring and training for the store. She is a mother of two girls. Her husband works on an oil rig and is home three times a year for one month each. Allison loves her job and has been a team player for the past three years. New employee hires have been reduced because she has decreased turnover by 50%.

Freddie is the Men's clothing and shoe department manager. He is married to Hank and they just adopted their first dog together. Freddie loves fashion and has been working to get the store more up to date. His degree is in management and he has been at the job for five years. Freddie wants more responsibility and eventually wants to be the store manager.

Evelyn is the Women's and Juniors' clothing department manager. She just transferred from another store six months ago, Evelyn is a single mother of a 14-year-old boy who just started high school. She works hard at her job but feels overwhelmed with the larger departments. She has been putting in extra hours each week to get the work accomplished.

Andy is the Children's and Home Goods manager. He has been with the business for 20 years at the same store. He is single and his job is his life. Since he has been doing the job for 20 years, change is difficult and sometimes causes delays in new stock. Andy wants to work his 30 years and retire.

You (the store manager) call a meeting to discuss sales goals and what has been going on in the store. You give your managers the facts and the information that corporate provided. You want to increase sales so that the store will not be shut down and your employees will keep their jobs. You work with your team to fix this problem.

Now, practice the scenario using the above instructions.

CONFLICT RESOLUTION

Handling conflict without escalating the situation into something worse is a very important skill. The critical factor in effective handling of conflict is to address the situation and not the person.

To attack the situation and not the person, the situation must be described as evenly and objectively as possible. The purpose of handling conflict is to resolve the conflict, not to vent emotion. If the confrontation has escalated to a level that is uncontrollable, it is best to try to address the situation later when the emotions have had some time to cool off.

Avoid accusatory "you" statements. Attack the situation and not the person. Even if the other person attacks you and attempts to escalate the conflict, you need to avoid a counterattack. Your purpose is to resolve the conflict.

There are six steps to KRT Conflict Resolution:

1. Find a quiet room and do not allow interruptions. Include all applicable parties who need to be there and participate in finding a resolution.
    a. Manager may be a mediator to help facilitate and make sure team stays on track
2. Describe what specifically and objectively happened to create conflict (person who brought up conflict/issue)
    a. Include relevant consequences
    b. Describe how you feel (brief statement)
    c. Describe how you think the other person sees the situation
3. Ask how the other team member(s) sees the situation
    a. Allow all parties to speak and not interrupt each other
    b. How do they feel
    c. Apply Active Listening (use steps)
4. Ask how to resolve
    a. Problem-solve (if needed)
    b. Proactive and positive focus on problem (not the person)

5. Agree on a resolution and seek commitment to resolve future conflicts
   a. Compromise on all parties may be required
6. End session with kindness
   a. Convey all parties involved are important
   b. End with a handshake/fist bump etc.

Conflict will occur, and we cannot shy away or run away from it. If the situation has escalated into a conflict, a lot of factors will play into how it is handled. Your choice of words and tone can make the other person defensive. If the person becomes defensive in step 1, then the result may be an exercise in futility. How you handle the conflict shows who you are a leader.

Conflict Resolution Example:

You are an employee at an IT business that specializes in cloud technology. You have been on the job for two years. Your manager tells you what a great job you are doing each day. But, every time a promotion comes up, you are not considered for the position.

Corina is your coworker. She has been at the business for three years. She also has been passed over promotions. She is ready to leave and wants you to come with her.

Ned is your boss. He has been with the business for ten years. He knows that you are a good employee. In fact, you get work done faster than other coworkers. Ned does not want to lose you from his team, so he does not put in your name for promotions.

You decide that you need to talk to Ned about the promotion and why you aren't even allowed to interview for the promotion.

Now, practice the scenario using the above instructions.

KRT Inaction—Example of what not to do

There was a conflict that my manager created by showing favoritism to a certain team of people. It was very blatant, and all teams saw what was going on and kept asking me about it. She would take the other team to lunch or just go hang out with them at lunch. She did not do this with any other team. Well, as you can imagine, this was starting to cause issues especially because that team was getting all the new projects (even though they had no idea what to do). I decided, for the sake of my team and my coworkers, I needed to address the situation.

I went in to speak with my manager concerning what was going on. I remained calm and collected when starting the meeting. When I started to explain the conflict, she could not acknowledge that there was a problem. She tried to gaslight me into thinking I was making up the scenario. She became defensive and angry. Her anger was pointed directly at me instead of the conflict that she had created. I should have stopped the conversation at this point—but I didn't. I took it personally and I started to get upset with my manager and all the issues that were occurring and that had been building up. This made her want to blame me more and there was no way the discussion was going to be constructive. At the end of the conversation, she was blaming me for all the issues and made herself the person who could do no wrong.

As you can imagine, the relationship between my manager and me became strained and was not productive at all. She changed my job description and title trying to set me up for failure. I went to Human Resources but, as discussed earlier, they did not care, didn't help, and told me to handle it myself.

This example illustrates how bad a conflict can become. Do not hold back conflicts, you need to face them head on and remember that it is not about the person, it's about the situation. Do not let your manager gaslight you and make you feel like it didn't happen. Document what is going on so that you have a record for Human Resources. Always be clear, concise, and straight to the point when handling these issues.

FEEDBACK

Feedback is defined as the direct information received by an individual concerning an action (such as work performance). When positive feedback is being given, the purpose is to provide reinforcement of the good behavior or performance. When negative feedback is being given, the purpose is to stress and express confidence in the other person. This allows the receiver to feel as though they have given confidence in that person to perform in the future. Giving feedback should be about helping the other person. Never use feedback to punish, belittle, yell at, or dominate the other person. Feedback should be used to develop the person not evaluate them. The person needs to know that you are deeply devoted to their development.

Giving KRT Feedback:

1. Find a quiet room and do not allow interruptions
2. State the behavior and consequences of the behavior
   a. Use clear and simple terms
3. Explain how you feel about the behavior

4. End session with kindness
   a. Give gratitude or express confidence
   b. Be sincere
   c. Make sure employee knows how important they are
   d. End with a handshake/fist bump etc.

Most people are hesitant to give any feedback (good or bad). They are afraid of negative responses. The result is missed opportunities for improvement and building of relationships. To get feedback, you may have to solicit the feedback. Think about the feedback as free consulting from the other person. Feedback is not an argument. Do not argue your side and do not attack the other person.

Receiving KRT Feedback:

1. Find a quiet room and do not allow interruptions
2. Seek more information for understanding
3. Paraphrase the feedback
   a. Don't be defensive if you disagree
4. Seek commitment for more feedback
5. End session with kindness
   a. Make sure manager/employee knows that you value their feedback
   b. End with handshake/fist bump etc.

Feedback can hurt your feelings but seek for understanding and the why behind the statements. Feedback helps us grow and evolve into leaders. Receiving negative feedback will happen, and it is up to you on how you handle it. Leaders learn and managers ignore.

Feedback Example:

You are a manager of a restaurant. The restaurant is open for lunch and dinner. Your team consists of three assistant managers over the kitchen, dining room, and bar. These managers do all of their own hiring and training. The managers are responsible for all aspects of their area including customers and money.

The restaurant has been reviewed over 1,000 times on Yelp and is considered very friendly with great food with a 4.5-star rating. Most nights are booked in advance and lunch has a steady crowd of businesspeople who work nearby.

Garrett is the manager over the kitchen. He has been at the restaurant for almost four years. He worked his way up from prep cook, to cook, to management. He has been a manager for the past year. Garrett is married with three children (two boys and one girl). He is a very good trainer and mentor for his team. He has been doing well and is learning more every day; you have confidence in his ability to do the job.

Hannah is the manager over the dining room. She has been in the restaurant business for a total of ten years with two being at the current job. She has been working her way through college part time in hospitality management. She is single and has friends at work. Hannah's goal is to be a restaurant manager one day. You know that Hannah knows her business and has made great improvements in dining room turnover.

Jose is the manager over the bar. He owned his own bar in Mexico and immigrated to the U.S. for a new beginning. His bar knowledge is amazing and he has saved the restaurant money by ordering differently from their suppliers. Jose is aggressive and wants to learn. Sometimes you must remind him to focus on the day-to-day operations of the bar. Jose just proposed to his girlfriend of two years.

Positive Feedback:

The food is always great in your restaurant. Recently, you have noticed that you have been getting more 5-star reviews because of the food. Garrett changed the menu to add in nightly specials. These specials are what the reviewers have been commenting about. Garrett has been taking specialty cooking classes in his off hours to learn more about his trade. You know that Garrett is behind the great reviews and you want to provide positive feedback.

Negative Feedback:

Hannah is the type of manager who wants to learn everything about the business. Her focus is on the dining room, but she helps out in the kitchen and bar areas. You notice that Hannah sometimes goes into the kitchen without washing her hands. This is a health concern and you want to avoid any health department violations. You want to talk with Hannah about this issue, but you don't want to discourage her from learning.

Now, practice the scenario using the above instructions.

6

BUSINESS CASE COST/BENEFIT MODEL

The **business case** provides justification for undertaking a project or program. It evaluates the benefit, cost, and risk of alternative options and provides a rationale for the preferred solution.

Business cases are created to help decision-makers ensure that:

1. The proposed initiative will have value and relative priority compared to alternative initiatives based on the objectives and expected benefits laid out in the business case.
2. The performance indicators found in the business case are identified to be used for proactive realization of the business and behavioral change.

People > Profit

There is no profit without your employees

All businesses want to make a profit. This is an easy truthful statement. How businesses make the profit is the hard part. Will the business pay livable wages? Will the business give a specific portion back to nonprofits and charities? Will the business conduct pay audits to prove equality? Will the business allow sexual harassment? Will the business keep high-performing Adult Bullies that suck all culture and happiness from their teams? These are all very real questions leaders should be asking.

I remember the day I got to help write my first business case. That day was not any different from any other stressful day, but it was informative. I learned very quickly that companies don't always look at the whole picture when they write their business cases, which causes failures that do not need to happen. I learned that the bottom line is king and paybacks needs to be ASAP. This is typical of most businesses. We want to make the improvements and see immediate results.

My business case was approved after just giving one presentation. We were making Average Handle Time (AHT) changes and updating the systems to make it easier for the employees on the phone. The fix should be cheap and easy with a huge payback. We got this update within one IT cycle. The employees were amazed at how fast we were able to get the change made. By moving quickly and stepping up to fix the problem, we gained the employees' respect and trust. These employees became more loyal and even quicker at their jobs due to the enhancements.

I have created or worked on dozens of business cases during my career with most getting funding and being implemented. I looked outside the box into the whole picture to find the issues and solutions. I talked to everyone who cared about the issue to talk through solutions. We always worked as a team for the common goal of making things easier for the employees' job and creating the best customer experience. This is how business thrives. This is how business grows.

Business cases have a basic structure and this book provided you with a Business Case for Kindness. We discussed what the problem is, in all of its complicated joy. We discussed the analysis of the problems and what the research reveals. Then we walked through solutions. Lastly, we are going to look at the cost benefit analysis.

When I started tackling how to create the Business Case for Kindness, I knew that this was the business case for the future. By making the changes needed and discussed in this book, organizations and businesses will be leading into the future of equality, equity, diversity, and inclusion. Anyone who doesn't make the changes needed will be left behind.

Did you know that office employees are only productive around three to five hours per shift? Did you know that retail and service industry workers are only productive for five out of an eight-hour shift? The average worker is only around 60% productive a day. That means 40% of the time they are not. We can try to blame all of this on technology or laziness, but that isn't the case. As you have learned repeatedly, we are our own worst enemy and we must make the changes needed. I really hope some of these numbers shock you and your company into immediate action. Don't you want to be the leader that transforms your organization or company? You can be. We all can be. You can be the one who goes to upper leadership stating, "Hey, I have this great idea that will dramatically increase our profits."

Cost and cost savings that will occur:

1. There will be a decrease in lawsuits if employers stop allowing the bad behaviors.
2. Employee retention will increase.
3. Customer retention will increase because employees will be treating customers better.
4. Employees will perform better at their jobs with increased productivity.
5. Companies should give a percentage to charity and nonprofits, which with the new mission, will increase customers.
6. There will be ongoing costs associated with the change (which will be higher in first few years due to fixing the wrongs we have discussed).

Assumptions on all examples:

- Per year
- Legal/Human Resources are 1% of all employees
- Turnover is 10% of all employees
- Customer retention is subjective and must be specific to your business
- Management is 10% of employees
- Customer acquisition is subjective and must be specific to your business

Example 1 Assumptions:

- 25% decrease in Legal/Human Resources due to less lawsuits (average cost $100,000 per year)

- 25% increase in retention of employees who would have left
- 50% increase in customer retention due to happier employees treating customers better
- 50% of employee base—30-minute productivity increase daily, $20 an hour (includes overhead), 52 weeks at five days a week
- 50% of management base—one-hour productivity increase daily, $35 an hour (includes overhead), 52 weeks at five days a week
- Additional customers due to new mission statement/better customer service
- Companies will give 20% of their new revenue ongoing to nonprofits and charities
- Cost to implement changes will be 25% of the savings each year

Company 1 (200,000+ employees)

	Total	#	$ increase revenue/saving	Savings per year
Legal/Human Resources	2,000	500	$100,000	$50,000,000
Employee Turnover (per year)	20,000	5,000	$5,000	$25,000,000
Customer Retention (per year)	200,000	100,000	$315	$31,500,000
Employee Productivity Increase	100,000	50,000	$2,600	$130,000,000
Manager Productivity Increase	100,000	50,000	$9,100	$455,000,000
Customer Acquisition (per year)	125,000		$6,000	$750,000,000
Total savings/earnings (per year)				**$1,441,500,000**
Additional Donations to Nonprofits and Charites				$288,300,000
Cost to Implement Changes				$360,375,000
Total Increased Earnings				**$792,825,000**

Example 2 Assumptions:

- 10% decrease in Legal/Human Resources due to less lawsuits (average cost $100,000 per year)
- 10% increase in retention of employees who would have left
- 25% increase in customer retention due to happier employees treating customers better
- 25% of employee base—30-minute productivity increases daily, $20 an hour (includes overhead), 52 weeks at five days a week
- 25% of management base—one-hour productivity increases daily, $35 an hour (includes overhead), 52 weeks at five days a week
- Additional customers due to new mission statement/better customer service
- Companies will give 20% of their new revenue ongoing to nonprofits and charities
- Cost to implement changes will be 50% of the savings each year

Company 2 (20,000 employees)

	Total	#	$ increase revenue/saving	Savings per year
Legal/Human Resources	200	20	$100,000	$3,000,000
Employee Turnover (per year)	2,000	200	$5,000	$1,000,000
Customer Retention (per year)	20,000	2,000	$315	$630,000
Employee Productivity Increase	18,000	4,500	$2,600	$11,700,000
Manager Productivity Increase	2,000	500	$9,100	$4,550,000
Customer Acquisition (per year)	100		$6,000	$600,000
Total Savings/Earnings (per year)				**$20,480,000**
Additional Donations to Nonprofits and Charites				$4,096,000
Cost to Implement Changes				$10,240,000
Total Increased Earnings				**$6,144,000**

Example 3 Assumptions:

- 20% decrease in Legal/Human Resources due to less lawsuits (average cost $100,000 per year)
- 20% increase in retention of employees who would have left
- 20% increase in customer retention due to happier employees treating customers better
- 10% of employee base—30-minute productivity increases daily, $20 an hour (includes overhead), 52 weeks at five days a week
- 10% of management base—one-hour productivity increases daily, $35 an hour (includes overhead), 52 weeks at five days a week
- Additional customers due to new mission statement/better customer service
- Companies will give 20% of their new revenue ongoing to nonprofits and charities
- Cost to implement changes will be 60% of the savings each year

Company 3 (2,000 employees)

	Total	#	$ increase revenue/saving	Savings per year
Legal/Human Resources	20	4	$100,000	$400,000
Employee Turnover (per year)	200	40	$5,000	$200,000
Customer Retention (per year)	1,000	200	$315	$63,000
Employee Productivity Increase	1,800	180	$2,600	$468,000
Manager Productivity Increase	200	20	$9,100	$182,000
Customer Acquisition (per year)	50		$6,000	$300,000
Total Savings/Earnings (per year)				**$1,613,000**
Additional Donations to Nonprofits and Charites				$322,600
Cost to Implement Changes				$967,800
Total Increased Earnings				**$342,600**

Example 4 Assumptions:

- 50,000 employees
- 5% decrease in Legal/Human Resources due to less lawsuits (average cost $100,000 per year)
- 20% increase in retention of employees who would have left
- 20% increase in customer retention due to happier employees treating customers better
- 50% of employee base—10-minute productivity increases daily, $20 an hour (includes overhead), 52 weeks at five days a week
- 50% of management base—15-minute productivity increases daily, $35 an hour (includes overhead), 52 weeks at five days a week
- Additional customers due to new mission statement/better customer service
- Companies will give 20% of their new revenue ongoing to nonprofits and charities
- Cost to implement changes will be 60% of the savings each year

Company 4 (50,000 employees)

	Total	#	$ increase revenue/saving	Savings per year
Legal/Human Resources	500	25	$100,000	$3,750,000
Employee Turnover (per year)	5,000	1,000	$5,000	$5,000,000
Customer Retention (per year)	2,000	400	$315	$126,000
Employee Productivity Increase	45,000	22,500	$867	$19,507,500
Manager Productivity Increase	5,000	2,500	$2,275	$5,687,500
Customer Acquisition (per year)	200		$6,000	$1,200,000
Total Savings/Earnings (per year)				**$ 34,021,000**
Additional Donations to Nonprofits and Charites				$ 6,804,200
Cost to Implement Changes				$ 20,412,600
Total Increased Earnings				**$ 6,804,200**

There will be many more cost-saving or revenue-generating effects when you make the changes covered in this book. Some include reduced number of managers due to less complaints, employees taking fewer sick days, and increased ideas from employees to help the company. Also, it is imperative that companies don't give all of this money back to the shareholders because, if you haven't been paying attention, that is part of the problem.

When you spread kindness then you will receive kindness. When you spread fear and intimidation you will receive unproductive and dissatisfied workers. This isn't rocket science. We have just lost our way. This change will not be instantaneous. It may be very difficult for a lot of companies, but in the end the strong companies who can face the truth and make the changes needed will be the ones who thrive.

Look, the numbers don't lie. Making the changes covered in this book will only bring positive results. Even if your company is smaller than the examples, the fact still remains that kindness will always lead to any company doing better. Are you ready to fight for the Business Case for Kindness?

Play around with your own
company information at
www.bekindtoall.com

7

NEXT STEPS—PUTTING IT ALL TOGETHER

When people to tell you to "pick your battles," what they are really are saying is, "don't rock the boat"— keep things the same. We have kept our mouths shut for way too long. *IT IS TIME WE ROCK THE F*CKING BOAT*

Employees (including managers, executives, and board members) have allowed ourselves to have a blind eye for too long on what is going on in business. Employees have kept their mouth shut because they are afraid of losing their job because no one was ever fired for being silent. Employees have dealt with the shame of all of this in private. Employees have not been rocking the boat. It's time to knock loose all the bad behaviors and let them drown in their own misery.

It is time that we voice our opinions and are heard instead of Human Resources gaslighting us. We can become more empathetic with more gratitude toward each other. We can hold businesses accountable for their actions while making the positive changes we need. We are the change.

The amazing kids at Marjory Stoneman Douglas High School in Parkland, Florida, and the new women in Congress are inspirations for more change. They are showing us that all of us can make a difference in our world. These changes need to happen at the local, state, and national level. I have said it before, we are at a pivotal turning point in our society. These changes aren't stopping…they are only growing bigger by the day.

"This bloody road remains a mystery. This sudden darkness fills the air. What are we waiting for? Won't anybody help us? What are we waiting for? We can't afford to be innocent. Stand up and face the enemy. It's a do-or-die situation—we will be invincible."

"Invincible" by Pat Benatar
Musician

Now is the time and invincible is the game. I am calling for everyone who believes in equity, equality, diversity, and inclusion to step up and be part of the solution. It is time that we Be Kind to All. It is time we stop allowing the greed to continue to ruin our country. It is time that we recognize and change our behavior—we are better than this.

We can stop the bad behaviors and Adult Bullies.

We can stop allowing all the discrimination, harassment, and retaliation.

We can recognize gaslighting and manipulative techniques.

We can recognize that stereotypes, bias, and how the media does affect us.

We can recognize that we do have a pay gap and a very large gap in income inequality.

We can lead with a mindset of inclusion.

We can stop misogyny, especially between women.

We can recognize that we do not have equity or equality, especially with women, LGBTQ+, and people of color.

We can recognize that Human Resources allows these issues and needs to change.

We can stop blaming the victim and letting the cheater win.

Millennials are our future and there is no going back. The future of business depends on us changing what we think a Leader is. Leaders come in all forms, including different colors and genders. Leaders will use the KRT model to both engage their employees and to be the leader that they/we need. This will lead to incredible customer service and employee satisfaction within their jobs.

Change is hard and there will be businesses who do not agree to facts and issues that I have raised. I say to you naysayers, "Start listening, watching, noticing what is going on around you. Not just in your social circles. You will be amazed by what you learn." Businesses have been passive for way too long, which makes it harder for them to change. It is up to both business and employees to keep evolving into better versions. ***Diversity will unleash our excellence.***

I want to be perfectly clear that what has been covered in this book is not a fad or some business practice that will be forgotten in two years. This is our future. Companies who don't step up and embrace the changes needed are doomed to fail. My favorite example of a company who is doing it right is VaynerMedia. They have a Chief Heart Officer whose job it is to help employees have a deeper sense of self, mediate conflict, and provide feedback. She does all of this on her platform of kindness, empathy, and true heart leadership.

What could you accomplish if you have the support of your management to try new things? You could unleash your employees' potential by taking away the roadblocks that companies have arbitrarily created. Imagine unlimited innovation and creativity because the team is not burdened by the fear of failure.

Caring about your employees is not weakness. It is time we stop striving to beat one another so we can make more money to buy more things. Buying more things will not make you happy. Trust me, money does not buy true happiness. You will not find true happiness until you are living a life that you can be proud of. Don't you want to get up each day happy and fulfilled instead of with stress and fear? It is possible for all of us.

By making the changes in this book for you, your team, and company, you will change. You will become more emotionally intelligent and happier. Your friends and family will notice. You will start to question things that maybe you never did before. This will show people it is ok to question the status quo. We have been led down a path of greed for too long and it's time we change our own narratives. It's time we step up to be the leaders that our world needs right now. The courage to do the right thing under overwhelming pressure, that is a sign of a great leader.

Before we end, have you thought about how you are going to implement what you learned in this book immediately? I would recommend you start with three things that you know you can implement today. For example, you could practice Active Listening, building kindness with an employee by encouraging them and speak up if you see a bad behavior. Write your three things down and make a commitment to yourself to do the work. I know change is hard and we allow being scared or fearful to hold us back. It's time we reframe these feelings into feelings of empowerment. We cannot allow the opinion of one person to paralyze us. We must say to ourselves: I feel nervous/scared and I love that feeling because it means I am growing and learning.

The evidence is clear and points us to the change that is coming. We need to embrace the future and make right all the things that went wrong. We can be the leaders we want to see. We can be the change in this world. We can be better than we are now. This is your chance to share what you have learned in this book and do your part in this historic movement in our history.

DO THE KIND THING

Share your three things at
www.bekindtoall.com/3things

REFERENCES

Introduction

Dickson, Caitlin. "How the U.S. Ended Up With 400,000 Untested Rape Kits." Daily Beast. April 14, 2017. https://www.thedailybeast.com/how-the-us-ended-up-with-400000-untested-rape-kits

McGregor, Jena. "Citigroup is revealing pay gap data most companies don't want to share." Washington Post. January 16, 2019. https://www.washingtonpost.com/business/2019/01/16/citigroup-is-revealing-pay-gap-data-most-companies-dont-want-share/?noredirect=on&utm_term=.765f1af89eed

Chapter 1

Anderson, Craig and Wayne Warburton. "The Impact of violent video games: an overview." Iowa State University. 2012. http://hdl.handle.net/1959.14/183570

Archer, Dale. "Violence, The Media and Your Brain." Psychology Today. September 2, 2013. https://www.psychologytoday.com/us/blog/reading-between-the-headlines/201309/violence-the-media-and-your-brain

Bogle, John. *Enough: True Measures of Money, Business, and Life.* New York: John Wiley & Sons Inc., 2009.

Brennan, Jordan. "The Oligarchy Economy: Concentrated Power, Income Inequality, and Slow Growth." Evonomics. April 11, 2016. www.evonomics.com/the-oligarchy-economy/

Brinded, Lianna. "Marc Benioff got tired of the gender pay gap at Salesforce, so he spent $3 million to close it—twice." Quartz. September 27, 2017. https://qz.com/1088328/salesforces-ceo-marc-benioff-ranks-in-ft-and-heroes-global-champion-of-women-in-business-list-for-eliminating-gender-pay-gap/

Campbell, Alexia Fernández. "9th Circuit: you can't pay women less than men just because they made less at their last job." Vox. April 10, 2018. https://www.vox.com/2018/4/10/17219158/equal-pay-day-2018

Cleary, Ekaterina Galkina, Jennifer M. Beierlein, Navleen Surjit Khanuja, Laura M. McNamee, and Fred D. Ledley. "Contribution of NIH funding to new drug approvals." Proceedings of the National Academy of Sciences (PNAS). March 6, 2018. https://www.pnas.org/content/115/10/2329

Donnelly, Grace. "Top CEOs Make More in Two Days Than An Average Employees Does In One Year." Fortune. July 20, 2017. https://fortune.com/2017/07/20/ceo-pay-ratio-2016/

Drutman, Lee. "How Corporate Lobbyists Conquered American Democracy." April 20, 2015. The Atlantic. https://www.theatlantic.com/business/archive/2015/04/how-corporate-lobbyists-conquered-american-democracy/390822/

Duffin, Erin. "Household income distribution in the United States in 2017." Statista. April 29, 2019. https://www.statista.com/statistics/203183/percentage-distribution-of-household-income-in-the-us/

Dunbar, John. "The 'Citizens United' Decision and Why It Matters." The Center for Public Integrity. October 18, 2012. https://publicintegrity.org/federal-politics/the-citizens-united-decision-and-why-it-matters/

Economy, Peter. "Why Are Millennials So Unhappy at Work?" Inc.com. February 4, 2016. http://www.inc.com/peter-economy/why-are-millennials-so-unhappy-at-work.html

Frankenfield, Jake. "Which Industry Spends the Most on Lobbying?" Investopedia. October 19, 2018. https://www.investopedia.com/investing/which-industry-spends-most-lobbying-antm-so/

Gaviola, Anne. "How Companies Are Dealing with Millennials Ghosting On their Jobs." Vice. October 10, 2018. https://free.vice.com/en_ca/article/yw9evk/how-companies-are-dealing-with-millennials-ghosting-on-their-jobs

Hatch, Jenavieve. "Federal Court Rules That Employers Can Pay A Woman Less As Long As Her Old Boss Did, Too." Huffpost. April 28, 2017. https://www.huffingtonpost.com/entry/federal-court-rules-that-employers-can-pay-a-woman-less-as-long-as-her-old-boss-did-too_us_5903435de4b0bb2d086d4481

Hern, Alex. "Fake news sharing in U.S. is a rightwing thing, says study." Guardian. February 6, 2018. https://www.theguardian.com/technology/2018/feb/06/sharing-fake-news-us-rightwing-study-trump-university-of-oxford

Illing, Sean. "How the baby boomers—not millennials—screwed America." Vox. December 20, 2017. https://www.vox.com/2017/12/20/16772670/baby-boomers-millennials-congress-debt

Indeed. "Report: How Satisfied Are U.S. Workers with Their Salaries?" http://blog.indeed.com/2018/01/25/salary-report/

Levin, Sam. "Google accused of 'extreme' gender pay discrimination by the U.S. labor department." The Guardian. April 7, 2017. https://www.theguardian.com/technology/2017/apr/07/google-pay-disparities-women-labor-department-lawsuit

Mervis, Jeffrey. "Data Check: U.S. government share of basic research funding falls below 50%" Science Magazine. March 9, 2017. https://www.sciencemag.org/news/2017/03/data-check-us-government-share-basic-research-funding-falls-below-50

Pandey, Erica. "Dollar stores thrive in distressed pockets of America." Axios. December 11, 2018. https://www.axios.com/rural-america-dollar-stores-retail-recession-grocery-51054373-38f8-45fd-b088-9ab0dd00aba3.html

Paquette, Danielle. "Court: Employers Can't Pay Women Less Because of Their Salary History." Washington Post. April 9, 2018. https://www.washingtonpost.com/news/wonk/wp/2018/04/09/court-employers-cant-pay-women-less-because-of-their-salary-history/?noredirect=on&utm_term=.bfeab3c05d88

Payscale. "CEO Pay: How Much Do CEOs Make Compared to their Employees?" https://www.payscale.com/data-packages/ceo-pay

Reich, Robert. *The Common Good.* New York: Alfred A. Knopf, 2018.

Ross, Jane. "California city fights poverty with guaranteed income." Reuters. June 4, 2018. https://www.reuters.com/article/us-california-income/california-city-fights-poverty-with-guaranteed-income-idUSKCN1J015D

Rubio, Marco. "America Needs to Restore Dignity of Work." The Atlantic. December 13, 2018. https://medium.com/the-atlantic/america-needs-to-restore-dignity-of-work-9fa5bf1ec738

Silverman, Craig. "This Analysis Shows How Viral Fake Election News Stories Outperformed Real News on Facebook." Buzzfeed News. November 16, 2016. https://www.buzzfeednews.com/article/craigsilverman/viral-fake-election-news-outperformed-real-news-on-facebook

U.S. Department of Health and Human Services, Office of the Assistant Secretary for Planning and Evaluation. "Poverty Guidelines." https://aspe.hhs.gov/2018-poverty-guidelines

Viviani, Nick. "EEOC sues KC pizza place over unequal pay for women." Associated Press. September 7, 2017. https://www.wibw.com/content/news/EEOC-sues-KC-pizza-place-for-unequal-pay-443015983.html

Wikipedia. Citizens United v. FEC. https://en.wikipedia.org/wiki/Citizens_United_

Wikipedia. "Second Bill of Rights." https://en.wikipedia.org/wiki/Second_Bill_of_Rights

Zaitchik, Alexander. "Taxpayers—not big Pharma—have funded the research behind every new drug since 2010." Other 98. March 2, 2018. https://other98.com/taxpayers-fund-pharma-research-development/

Chapter 2

Adams, Scott. *The Dilbert Principle: A Cubicle's-Eye View of Bosses, Meetings, Management Fads & Other Workplace Afflictions.* New York: Harper Business, 1996.

Alter, Charlotte. "What Trans Men See that Women Don't." Time. http://time.com/transgender-men-sexism/

Bassett, Laura. "The U.N. Sent 3 Foreign Women to the U.S. to Assess Gender Equality. They Were Horrified." Huffington Post. December 15, 2015. http://www.huffingtonpost.com/entry/foreign-women-assess-us-gender-equality_us_566ef77de4b0e292150e92f0?section=politics

Berlinski, Claire. "The Warlock Hunt," The American Interest. December 6, 2017. https://www.the-american-interest.com/2017/12/06/the-warlock-hunt/

Bookbinder, Dave. "Toxic Workers Are More Productive, But the Price Is High." TLNT. April 20, 2018. https://www.tlnt.com/toxic-workers-are-more-productive-but-the-price-is-high/

Brescoll, Victoria L. and Eric Luis Uhlmann. "Can Angry Woman Get Ahead?: Status Conferral, Gender, and Expression of Emotion in the Workplace." Harvard Kennedy School. http://gap.hks.harvard.edu/can-angry-woman-get-ahead-status-conferral-gender-and-expression-emotion-workplace

Bullying Statistics. Bullyingstatistics.org

CBS News. "'A Cultural Rot': Sex assaults spike at U.S. service academies." February 1, 2019. https://www.cbsnews.com/news/sexual-assault-reports-at-military-academies-spiked-last-academic-year-pentagon-report/

Chira, Susan and Brianna Milord. "Is There a Man I Can Talk To?: Stories of Sexism in the Workplace." New York Times, June 20, 2017. https://www.nytimes.com/2017/06/20/business/women-react-to-sexism-in-the-workplace.html

CNN Wire Service. "Only these 8 states require sex education classes to mention consent." CNN. September 29, 2018. https://fox6now.com/2018/09/29/only-these-8-states-require-sex-education-classes-to-mention-consent/

Cooper, Sarah. "9 Non-Threatening Leadership Strategies for women." Cooper Review. July 27, 2016. http://thecooperreview.com/non-threatening-leadership-strategies-for-women/

Dishman, Lydia. "60% of Women in Silicon Valley Have Been Sexually Harassed." Fast Company. January 1, 2016. https://www.fastcompany.com/3055395/60-of-women-in-silicon-valley-have-been-sexually-harassed

Duggan, Maeve. "Online Harassment 2017." Pew Research. July 11, 2017. https://www.pewinternet.org/2017/07/11/online-harassment-2017/

Evans, Gail. *Play Like a Man, Win Like a Woman.* Broadway Books. 2000.

Feldberg, Alexandra C. and Tami Kim. "Beyond Starbucks: How Racism Shapes Customer Service." New York Times. April 20. 2018. https://www.nytimes.com/2018/04/20/opinion/starbucks-racism-customer-service.html

Fessler, Leah. "Men who want to fight sexism at work: Read Sheryl Sandberg's blunt advice," Quartz. August 31, 2017. https://work.qz.com/1065929/read-sheryl-sandbergs-blunt-advice-to-men-who-want-to-fight-sexism-at-work/

Fessler, Leah. "We tested bots like Siri and Alexa to see who would stand up to sexual harassment." Quartz. February 22, 2017. https://qz.com/911681/we-tested-apples-siri-amazon-echos-alexa-microsofts-cortana-and-googles-google-home-to-see-which-personal-assistant-bots-stand-up-for-themselves-in-the-face-of-sexual-harassment/

Healthy Workplace Campaign. http://healthyworkplacebill.org/

Kozuch, Elliott. "HRC Releases Annual Corporate Equality Index with Record 609 Companies Earning Perfect Scores" Human Rights Campaign. 2018. https://www.hrc.org/blog/hrc-releases-annual-corporate-equality-index-609-companies-earn-perfect-sco

Lane, Christopher. "The Stress of Discrimination in the U.S." Psychology Today. March 11, 2016. https://www.psychologytoday.com/us/blog/side-effects/201603/the-stress-discrimination-in-the-us

LaVito, Angelica. "Nike CEO apologizes to employees for workplace culture after months of turmoil." CNBC. May 4, 2018. https://www.

cnbc.com/2018/05/04/nike-ceo-apologizes-to-employees-for-workplace-culture-after-months-of-turmoil.html

Lean In. Women in the Workplace 2017. https://womenintheworkplace.com/2017

Lemmon, Gayle Tzemach. "'I'm Not Your Wife!' A New Study Points to a Hidden Form of Sexism." The Atlantic. June 5, 2012. https://www.theatlantic.com/national/archive/2012/06/im-not-your-wife-a-new-study-points-to-a-hidden-form-of-sexism/258057/

Mallon, Maggie. "Here's How Frequently Women Supreme Court Justices Are Interrupted By Men." Glamour. April 6, 2017. https://www.glamour.com/story/how-frequently-women-supreme-court-justices-are-interrupted-by-men

Malmstrom, Malin, Jeaneth Johansson, and Joakim Wincent. "We Recorded VCs' Conversations and Analyzed How Differently They Talk About Female Entrepreneurs." Harvard Business Review. May 17, 2017. https://hbr.org/2017/05/we-recorded-vcs-conversations-and-analyzed-how-differently-they-talk-about-female-entrepreneurs

Marcin, Tim. "Nearly 60 Percent of Republicans Don't Want a Woman President in Their Lifetime, Poll Finds." Newsweek. April 26, 2018. https://www.newsweek.com/nearly-60-percent-republicans-dont-want-woman-president-lifetime-poll-902254

Maurer, Roy. "Workplace-Bullying Laws on the Horizon." SHRM. July 16, 2013. https://shrm.org/ResourcesAndTools/hr-topics/risk-management/Pages/Workplace-Bullying-Laws.aspx

Merchant, Nilofer. "The Insidious Economic Impact of Sexual Harassment." Harvard Business Review. November 29, 2017. https://hbr.org/2017/11/the-insidious-economic-impact-of-sexual-harassment

Merkin, Daphne. "Publicly, We Say #MeToo. Privately, We Have Misgivings." The New York Times, January 5, 2018. https://www.nytimes.com/2018/01/05/opinion/golden-globes-metoo.html

Peck, Emily. "Well-Off White Men Are 3 Times More Likely Than Women To Get Job Interviews." Huffington Post. January 5, 2017.

https://www.huffingtonpost.ca/entry/women-motherhood-penalty_
n_586d69fae4b0c4be0af2c02c

Polk, Sam. "How Wall Street Bro Talk Keeps Women Down," The
New York Times. July 10, 2016. https://www.nytimes.com/2016/
07/10/opinion/sunday/how-wall-street-bro-talk-keeps-women-
down.html?_r=0

Reinstein, Julia. "This Teen Says Her Chili's Manager Sexually Harassed
Her, and Her Coworkers Threw a Party To Shame Her," BuzzFeed.
April 5, 2017. https://www.buzzfeed.com/juliareinstein/this-teen-
reported-her-chilis-manager-for-sexual-harassment?utm_term=.
ucxPlk5DJ#.cf9DLPadK

Safe Horizon. "Domestic Violence." https://www.safehorizon.org/get-
informed/domestic-violence-statistics-facts/#statistics-and-facts/

Sarachit, Jaime. "Today is Equal Pay Day. So, If You're a Woman Asking
for More Money, Think Like a Man. Just Don't Act Like One."
Women Entrepreneur. April 10, 2018. https://www.entrepreneur.
com/article/311684

Sarkis, Stephanie. "Gaslighting: Know it and identify it to protect
yourself." Psychology Today. January 22, 2017. https://www.psy-
chologytoday.com/blog/here-there-and-everywhere/201701/
gaslighting-know-it-and-identify-it-protect-yourself

Schlessinger, Laura. *The Proper Care and Feeding of Husbands*. Harper.
2004.

Solomon, Kristine. "A Cheerleader is Suing Her School After They Tried
to Cover Up Her Sexual Assault." Yahoo. January 24, 2017. https://
www.yahoo.com/lifestyle/a-cheerleader-is-suing-her-school-after-
they-tried-to-cover-up-her-sexual-assault-054604010.html

Stanley, Andrea. "The Anti-Defamation League Issues Its First-Ever
Report Tying Misogyny to White Supremacy." Cosmopolitan.
July 24, 2018. https://www.cosmopolitan.com/politics/a22516345/
anti-defamation-league-white-supremacy-misogyny/

Swartz, John and Mary Nahorniak. "The 'elephant in the Valley' is tech's
problem." USA Today. March 13, 2016. https://www.usatoday.com/
story/tech/2016/03/13/elephant-valley-sxsw/81736732/

Swartz, Mark. "How to Reduce Stereotyping In The Workplace." Monster.com. https://www.monster.ca/career-advice/article/overcoming-workplace-stereotyping

Tippett, Elizabeth C. "Opinion: Nike's #MeToo moment shows a better approach to tackling sexual harassment." MarketWatch. May 4, 2018. https://www.marketwatch.com/story/nikes-metoo-moment-shows-a-better-approach-to-tackling-sexual-harassment-2018-05-02

Turban, Stephen, Laura Freeman, and Ben Waber. "A Study Used Sensors to Show That Men and Women are Treated Differently at Work." Harvard Business Review. October 23, 2017. https://hbr.org/2017/10/a-study-used-sensors-to-show-that-men-and-women-are-treated-differently-at-work

University of Michigan. "How do Male Executives React When a Woman or Minority Becomes CEO? Not Great, According to New Research." Ross School of Business. February 15, 2018. https://michiganross.umich.edu/rtia-articles/how-do-male-executives-react-when-woman-or-minority-becomes-ceo-not-great-according

U.S. Equal Employment Opportunity Commission. "Holistic Approach Needed to Change Workplace Culture to Prevent Harassment, Experts Tell EEOC." October 31, 2018. https://www.eeoc.gov/eeoc/newsroom/release/10-31-18.cfm

Vagianos, Alanna. "2 Men Cleared of Rape After Italian Court Ruled Woman 'Too Masculine' To Be Attacked." Huffington Post. March 12, 2019. https://www.huffingtonpost.in/entry/italy-rape-case-too-masculine_in_5c88860fe4b0fbd7661ef541

Weiss, Suzannah. "5 Oppressive Tactics We Need To Stop Using in Our Anti-Oppression Work," Everyday Feminism, December 12, 2016. http://everydayfeminism.com/2016/12/oppressive-anti-oppressive-rhetoric/

Workplace Bullying Institute. www.workplacebullying.org/

Young, Damon. "Men Just Don't Trust Women—And It's a Huge Problem." Huffington Post. March 16, 2015. http://www.huffingtonpost.com/damon-young/men-just-dont-trust-women_b_6714280.html

Chapter 3

Blanchard, Ken and Barbara Glanz. *The Simple Truths of Service: Inspired by Johnny the Bagger*. McMillan Media and Simple Truths LLC. 2005.

Collins, Jim. *Good to Great: Why Some Companies Make the Leap…And Others Don't*. Harper Business. 2001.

Feldberg, Alexandra C. and Tami Kim. "Beyond Starbucks: How Racism Shapes Customer Service." The New York Times, April 20. 2018. https://www.nytimes.com/2018/04/20/opinion/starbucks-racism-customer-service.html

Ghosh, Soma. "What to Do When Your Boss Is a Nightmare." Thrive Global. August 20, 2018. https://thriveglobal.com/stories/what-to-do-when-your-boss-is-a-nightmare/

Gregoire, Carolyn. "How Your Toxic Boss Is Hurting Your Mental Health," Huffington Post. January 10, 2017. http://www.huffingtonpost.com/entry/bad-boss-mental-health_us_5873b3fee4b043ad97e4a444

Powers, Kirsten. "Americans are depressed and suicidal because something is wrong with our culture." USA Today. June 9, 2018, https://www.usatoday.com/story/opinion/2018/06/09/kate-spade-suicide-anthony-bourdain-depression-culture-success-column/687388002/

ACKNOWLEDGMENTS

The journey of creating this book has been amazing. I spent the past four years researching, talking to tens of thousands of people, and becoming active in my community. In 2015, when I quit my job, I never would have believed that a man whose businesses went bankrupt and was known for stiffing his workers would become our 45th president. But that is the world we are living in as of 2019. It is up to us to be the change. We are the leaders we have been looking for.

I want to thank everyone who helped me along this path. Making a career change is always challenging, but with great friends and chosen family I have been able to make my dream a reality. By telling the truth and facing the harsh realities, we can all make the change we wish to see in this world.

"Be the leader tomorrow needs."

—Cherie Crim
Author and Leadership Expert

ABOUT THE AUTHOR

Cherie Crim is the Founder and CEO of Be Kind to All, a consulting, training, and coaching kindness company focused on ending discrimination—in all of its forms—in today's business world. A resident of Panama City Beach, Florida, she is a founding board member of the first safe space for LGBTQ youth and is a candidate for City Council (2020). Cherie is a thought leader, activist, and truth teller who knows that kindness is the path forward. She is available for speaking, consulting, and coaching engagements. To learn more visit BeKindToAll.com

CPSIA information can be obtained
at www.ICGtesting.com
Printed in the USA
LVHW070254110920
665681LV00029BA/159